John

LIGHTHOUSES OF THE EAST COAST
East Anglia and Lincolnshire

ROBIN JONES

HALSGROVE

First published in Great Britain in 2013.

Title page: *All out to sea but only just: Dovercourt Low Lighthouse.* DAVID WHITTLE

To Jenny, Ross and Vicky

British Library Cataloguing-in-Publication Data
A CIP record for this title is available from the British Library

ISBN 978 0 85704 167 8

HALSGROVE
Halsgrove House,
Ryelands Business Park,
Bagley Road, Wellington, Somerset TA21 9PZ
Tel: 01823 653777   Fax: 01823 216796
email: sales@halsgrove.com

Part of the Halsgrove group of companies
Information on all Halsgrove titles is available at: www.halsgrove.com

Printed in China by Everbest Printing Co Ltd

CONTENTS

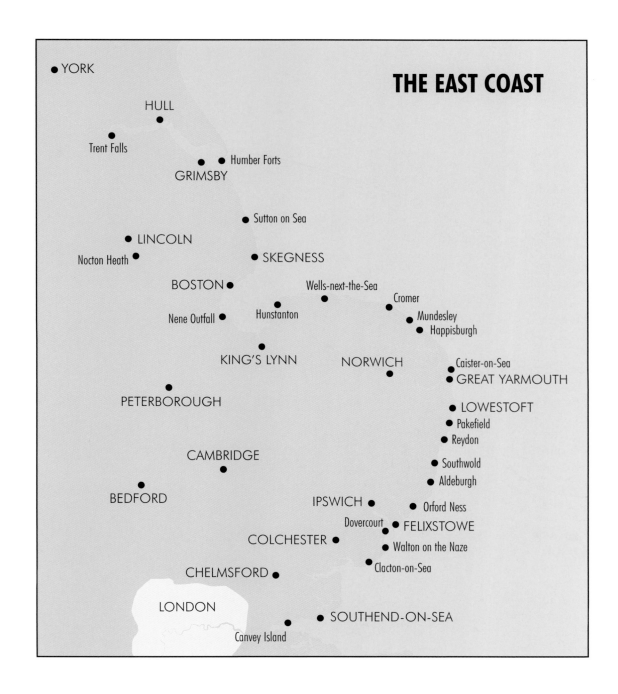

THE EAST COAST

YORK

HULL

Trent Falls

Humber Forts

GRIMSBY

Sutton on Sea

LINCOLN

Nocton Heath

SKEGNESS

BOSTON

Wells-next-the-Sea

Cromer

Nene Outfall

Hunstanton

Mundesley

Happisburgh

KING'S LYNN

NORWICH

Caister-on-Sea

GREAT YARMOUTH

PETERBOROUGH

LOWESTOFT

Pakefield

Reydon

CAMBRIDGE

Southwold

Aldeburgh

BEDFORD

IPSWICH

Orford Ness

Dovercourt

FELIXSTOWE

COLCHESTER

Walton on the Naze

Clacton-on-Sea

CHELMSFORD

LONDON

SOUTHEND-ON-SEA

Canvey Island

INTRODUCTION

THE SMOOTH ROUNDED coastline of East Anglia and its northern neighbour Lincolnshire lie on the opposite side of England from the jagged shore of the south-west peninsula, yet their shapes make them seem a world apart.

In my Halsgrove book *Lighthouses of the South West*, I explored how the coasts of Devon, Cornwall and the Isles of Scilly were particularly treacherous, with razor-sharp rocks lurking beneath merciless headlands which lay on the major shipping routes around Land's End.

The coasts of East Anglia and Lincolnshire are much lower by comparison, yet there are equally deadly menaces lurking in the waters that lie off them.

The key here is the natural processes of coastal erosion which have given Norfolk and Suffolk their distinctive shape on the map. Waves eat into cliffs, greedily taking away the spoil from the landslips from the ensuing cliff falls. Accordingly, the shore recedes, and whole towns, never mind lighthouses built to guard these shores, disappear beneath the waves forever.

At the same time, the debris collected by the sea must end up somewhere, and it is usually deposited a few miles further along the coast, or in sandbanks built up out to sea often where many centuries ago there had been dry land. Coastal erosion is a 24/7 process, and what might be a deepwater channel between these sandbanks leading to a thriving harbour at one time may have changed course completely within only a few years, or have become silted up altogether.

Navigational aids here are just as vital in saving lives as their counterparts on the unforgiving granite coasts of Cornwall. In East Anglia and Lincolnshire, there is no Land's End equivalent as such, but the busy historic sea route to be protected is that from Tyneside to the Port of London. In the days before railways, coastal shipping provided the most efficient and cost-effective means of bulk trade between the north and south, and it was vital that the sea lanes were made as safe as possible.

Necessity leads to invention and innovation, and it was on this coast that major advancements in world lighthouse technology took place.

Against this background of scientific progress was the constant feuding between private entrepreneurs, who saw lighthouses as a means of becoming rich by imposing dues on passing

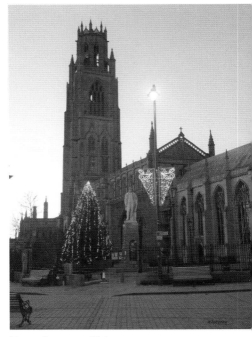

Boston Stump at Christmas.

5

ships, and the lighthouse authority for England and Wales, Trinity House, which jealously wanted to protect such rights for itself.

In several cases Trinity House would argue that there was no need for a lighthouse along a stretch of coast despite wreck statistics, and laughed off the pioneering enterprise which saw the world's first lightship established at the Nore at the mouth of the Thames estuary midway between Essex and Kent in 1731, not taking up the technology itself for another six decades despite its resounding success.

In addition to the land lighthouses covered in this volume, there grew a flotilla of lightships which protected the sea lanes way off shore, with names like Sunk Centre, Smiths Knoll, Cork, Newarp and Inner Dowsing.

There are many other world firsts in these pages, of which both the region and the country can be justifiably proud. Lowestoft lighthouse can boast that, wartime apart, it has shone continuously for more than four centuries and is the longest-established in Great Britain still in regular service.

Opposite: Dovercourt's High lighthouse high and dry on the sands. DAVID WHITTLE

Southwold lighthouse. ROBIN JONES

7

Lighthouses are often seen as a candy-striped tower which forms part of any good seaside resort's coastal furniture. Indeed, we have a classic example of an 'archetypal' traditional lighthouse tower painted in alternating red and white striped bands at Happisburgh. But as this book will highlight, they come in all shapes and sizes, from the lofty town trademark that is Southwold's gleaming white lighthouse to the street lamp fixed to the roof of the Marconi Sailing Club's headquarters on the River Blackwater. Also, they do not have to be beside the sea: Lincolnshire's curious Nocton Heath lighthouse is Britain's most famous inland version, more than 20 miles from the nearest coast and not a ship in sight.

What I have found most fascinating of all in writing this volume are the great stories behind, or associated with, each lighthouse.

The lightship that acquired fame as a pirate radio vessel. The fowler who, while living in a Lincolnshire lighthouse, underwent a conversion on the road to Damascus and changed from killing birds for meat to becoming one of the world's leading conservationists of all time. The Regency aristocrat who combined his philandering obsession with sex orgies with philanthropy in building a lighthouse to make the way home safer for travellers.

Then there was the lighthouse keeper who was found working as a barman in a nearby pub while he should have been on duty, the experimental lighthouses where the great scientist Michael Faraday carried out tests, and the lightship that was infamously machine gunned by the Luftwaffe early in World War Two with tragic consequences and alerted the British population to the fact we were not exactly dealing with a jolly good sort on the continent.

Some of the structures featured here were not built as lighthouses, but became navigational aids nonetheless. The towering Boston Stump was a classic example of an early "ecclesiastical light" whereby a candle was placed at a window as a simple aid to medieval mariners. Bateman's Tower at Brightlingsea was built by a man in order to help his daughter recover from tuberculosis.

Meanwhile, Grimsby's great Dock Tower was designed partly as a lighthouse but never used as such – although grateful Nazi bomber pilots left it alone as they used it as a navigational aid on their way to England's northern cities.

Lighthouses, lightships and light buoys are now automatic, and all of those in England and Wales are controlled remotely from a single hub, the Trinity House operations centre in Harwich, which has a chapter of its own. Several of them have been switched off permanently, or are in danger of being made redundant, because of the huge advances in satellite navigation technology in recent times.

There are those, however, who have their doubts. What happens where a local fisherman finds that his Global Positioning System device has suddenly stopped working? What would happen if a fault developed with the network in a 'black spot'?

Such is the strength of feeling that when Happisburgh's lighthouse was declared redundant, locals obtained statutory powers to take it over and run it by themselves.

Opposite: This statue of a wolf now guards the arched ruins of St Edmund's chapel, an early ecclesiastical light centuries later superseded by Hunstanton lighthouse, which lays claim to having been home to the world's first parabolic reflector, and is now used as holiday accommodation. Legend has it that after St Edmund was captured and decapitated by the Danes, a loyal wolf stood guard over his head until his friends could find it and bury it along with the rest of his body. ROBIN JONES

Standing sentinel over a modern industrial landscape are the very unalike twins of Killingholme High and Low Lights, which guide ships along the River Humber.
ROBIN JONES

Lighthouses today are a threatened species. The process of replacement by man combined with the permanent threat of coastal erosion has seen many of them on this coast already lost – Happisburgh Low Light, Mucking Bight, Tilburyness, Lowestoft Low Light and Landguard Point to name a few that have vanished, and with the encroachment of the sea, even much-loved landmarks like Orfordness lighthouse may soon follow.

CHAPTER ONE
TRENT FALLS

TRENT FALLS IS NOT NIAGARA – in fact, it is a diametric opposite.

At the confluence where the River Trent and the Yorkshire Ouse meet to form the Humber, there are no 'real' waterfalls as such, but a rapid race of water at tricky states of the tide. The flood tide funnelled up the Trent at certain times of the year creates a tidal bore known as the Trent Aegir, similar to the better-known Severn Bore.

Trent Falls as seen from Alkborough, a village at the north-western extremity of Lincolnshire. By a quirk of the Alkborough & Walcot parish boundary, the Trent Falls light lies within it, despite the structure being 'attached' to the opposite and Yorkshire bank of the Trent, and inaccessible from Alkborough village. ROBIN JONES

Above: *Apex Light at high tide in 1974.* DR NEIL CLIFTON*

Above right: *The Apex lighthouse at low tide.* YWM

Right: *The modern beacon which replaced the Apex lighthouse.* SAM ROEBUCK*

Just before the rivers meet, the Trent curves to the east in a manmade realignment. After World War One, a training wall was built on the river's western bank in a bid to stabilise the navigable channel.

The Trent deposits vast amounts of silt at this point, and charts for coastal shipping need to be updated on a monthly basis.

The rapids can make navigation difficult, with boats often having to wait for several hours until the flood tide carries them back upstream.

At the end of the training wall, a lighthouse known as Apex Light was built in 1933 to improve navigation.

The lighthouse, a red-painted 40ft steel structure erected on wooden pile foundations, was owned by the Lower Ouse Improvement Trustees, although it came within the bounds of the Humber Conservancy Board.

Its light was powered by electricity supplied from the trustees' own generating station at Blacktoft, with an acetylene gas back-up.

With a focal plane of 30ft above high water, the light had fourth order dioptric group triple flashing. A ten-second sequence comprised half a second light, one second eclipse, half a second light, one second eclipse, half a second light, following by six-and-a-half seconds eclipse.

It showed white for entering the Trent and red for entering the Ouse.

A diaphone foghorn in the structure ran on electrically compressed air and emitted a 1¾-second blast every 12 seconds. As back-up, there was an electric siren.

The whole installation was controlled by the pier master at Blacktoft Jetty.

Blacktoft Sands is now owned by Associated British Ports which has leased it to the Royal Society for the Protection of Birds.

As a nature reserve, it is of national importance. Bordering the training wall, it includes 480 acres of reed bed, estuarine mud and open water, and is visited by 270 species of birds, including breeding pairs of bearded tits, bitterns and marsh harriers.

The Apex Light has been moved upstream – to a new permanent home at the Yorkshire Waterways Museum in Goole. The museum, which stands on the side of the Dutch River, also includes a large fleet of boats, and admission is free.

The lighthouse has been replaced by a basic navigational light mast on the old Blacktoft Jetty.

Above: *The Apex Light from Trent Falls at the Yorkshire Waterways Museum in Goole. It now stands guard over a model boat pond.* ROBIN JONES

Below left: *Located in the Humber at Upper Whitton off the northern tip of Lincolnshire, downstream from Trent Falls, is this red-painted 'light float', a lightship in miniature. A 30ft square skeletal tower stands on a 33ft hull. Its focal plane is around 30ft.* MARTIN WRIGHT*

Below right: *The Yorkshire Waterways Museum at Goole.* YWM

CHAPTER TWO
THE KILLINGHOLME TRIO

THREE CLASSIC LIGHTHOUSES exist in close proximity at Killingholme on the south bank of the Humber.

They were erected to guide ships along this busy sea lane, and partner the sister lighthouse at Paull in Yorkshire on the north bank.

Their story begins in 1369, when the Guild of the Holy Trinity was instituted at Hull.

This institution is to the Humber what Trinity House in London is to the rest of the coast, a supreme maritime authority.

Back in the fourteenth century, Hull sailors were renowned for their seamanship. In *The Canterbury Tales*, Geoffrey Chaucer introduces the character of the Shipman who is described as "Ther was non such from Hull to Cartage" (Carthage).

The guild was granted privilege by Henry VI in 1443 and in 1457 it was incorporated by royal charter. The same year, an almshouse was founded in Hull for poor mariners, financed by the dues from shipping fees.

Charles II turned the guild into a corporation, with twelve "elder brethren" and six assistants, with the younger brethren comprising masters and pilot seamen.

The first elder brethren were nominated by the king. Among their many powers was the right to place buoys and beacons in the Humber for navigation, as well as the licensing of the pilots.

In 1828, the brethren wrote to the vicar of St Denys's church at Killingholme, asking him to cut down trees in front of the building which were preventing it from being used as a sea mark. He was threatened with a £100 fine.

The vicar said that no trees belonging to the church blocked the navigational view of the tower.

The trees were found to belong to neighbours Joseph Wright and Thomas Nicholson, who agreed to remove them.

The brethren, however, were back seven years later, this time demanding that the church tower should be whitewashed, the cost of which was £7, in order to emphasise its prominence as a daymark.

In June 1836, the brethren decided to build fully-fledged lighthouses at Killingholme.

Above left: *Killingholme High Light, still giving sterling service today.* ROBIN JONES
Above right: *Killingholme Low Light, with the High Light behind it.* ROBIN JONES

Above right and below: *Now a private house, Killingworth North Low Light has not shone a light since 1920.* ROBIN JONES

They bought land from David Brockley for £105 and commissioned William Hearfield to build two circular brick lighthouses to the design of Francis Dales for £350. They were designated the High Light and the Low Light.

The 50ft tall High Light was built from brick coated with cement in 1836. Its fixed bright light was produced by burning rapeseed oil. The first keeper was Samuel Pape, who was paid £50 a year and given a cottage next to the lighthouse to live in.

Complaints from shipmasters in 1845 that the small difference in height between the High and Low Lights was causing them problems led to the High Light being raised by 20ft, and the lamps in both improved.

The High Light was painted red in 1860 to make it stand out more.

The lantern was of the catoptric type, with three lamps, and showed a fixed white light visible for 14 miles.

On 21 September 1868, the son of keeper Thomas Leaper accidentally fell from thee lighthouse and died.

The High Light was struck by lightning on 4 June 1875 and the lantern was partially ripped away. The surveyor who came to inspect the damage recommended that it should be taken down and rebuilt, and the stonework was already decaying.

The replacement lighthouse was 78ft high, being built of red bricks covered in concrete, with a new cottage attached. Two temporary lighthouses on specially-built jetties on the shore held the fort until the first light was shone in the new High Light in December 1876.

In 1908, the Humber Conservancy Board was established and the lighthouse was transferred to it from Trinity House at Hull. It passed to the Port of Grimsby, now part of Associated British Ports.

New light apparatus fuelled by vapourised petroleum and operated by a clockwork mechanism driven by a falling weight contained in a metal tube in the centre of the lighthouse was installed in 1920.

The High Light is still operational today, but the keeper's cottage has long since gone. Grade II listed by English Heritage, the four-storey High Light is now enclosed in the grounds of one of Killingholme's two oil refineries.

With a 69ft focal plane, the red light occults once every four seconds.

The High Light stands about 630ft west of the Low Light, which stands 45ft high and also dates from 1836.

Rapeseed oil was also used to illuminate the fixed white bright light shone by the catoptric lantern which had two lamps, and could be seen for 11 miles.

However, the first keeper, Robert Brocklesby, who lived in the cottage attached to the lighthouse, complained after two years that the smoke rendered it all but inhabitable.

The brethren decided to rebuild the cottage, but then changed their minds, simply adding another storey to the existing one and raising the chimney to the level of the light, thereby curing the problem.

The Low Light was painted white in 1860 to make it more distinguishable.

Also run by the Port of Grimsby, the Low Light is similarly enclosed by the oil refinery fence today.

The disused North Low Light dates from 1851, when the brethren decided an extra one was needed at Killingholme. They hired William Foale to draw up plans and Hutchinson & Musgrave of Hull to build a brick circular 46ft tower to the north of the High Light. It first shone its light in 1852, and it was originally used as a signal station for the huge number of trawlers and fishing vessels entering what was once the biggest fishing port in the world.

By the early years of the twentieth century, the Humber channels had moved, and the North Low Light was no longer accurate.

It closed on 20 April 1920, and became used as living accommodation for the High Light keeper.

Now a private residence and also a Grade II listed building, the lighthouse is in a good

The first navigational aid to mariners in Killingholme was the tower of St Denys's church. DAVID WRIGHT*

state of preservation, having been restored in 2003, and is now protected by a concrete flood wall defensive barrier. An extra storey has been added to the keeper's cottage, the only one surviving at Killingholme.

It is possible to walk along the sea wall and inspect all three lighthouses from the path, but none of them are open to the public.

Killingholme is today a rapidly-growing port in its own right. It handles roll-on-roll-off ferries from Belgium and The Netherlands, and car imports both from the continent and South Korea.

During World War Two, RAF 550 Squadron flew Lancaster bombers from North Killingholme airbase from early 1944 to October 1945, and opened the D-day attack on 5 June 1944.

The parish contained two villages, North Killingholme, which includes St Denys's church, and the larger South Killingholme. It also encompasses Immingham power station, the Immingham Coal Terminal, the Humber International Terminal, most of the Associated Petroleum Terminals and the Immingham Ore Terminal.

Some of the huge vessels to be seen in the Humber shipping lanes past Killingholme today. ROBIN JONES

CHAPTER THREE
GRIMSBY DOCK TOWER

IT SURPRISES MANY THAT a major port like Grimsby does not have a lighthouse. Yet one was built for the town, and remains its most prominent landmark.

This enigma comes about from the fact that Grimsby Dock Tower was designed both as a lighthouse and as a hydraulic accumulator tower, but served only the latter purpose. It was decided that the 309ft fall tower would confuse mariners with the lights at Spurn Head on the opposite bank of the Humber estuary.

A hydraulic accumulator tower is designed to provide hydraulic power, in this instance, to operate the harbour's lock gates and 15 cranes.

The Dock Tower contains a 30,000-gallon wrought iron reservoir 247ft up – the extreme height being necessary to achieve sufficient water pressure to operate machinery, as opposed to merely provide a water supply, as is the case with most water towers. Incidentally, the Dock Tower also supplied water to the local area, the water being extracted from a well.

Grimsby Dock Company was formed to develop a commercial dock and fish dock, and building began in 1849, a year after the Manchester, Sheffield & Lincolnshire and East Lincolnshire railways arrived in the town and after a massive coffer dam one-and-a-half miles long was built. Prince Albert laid the foundation stone for the new dock wall and the construction on which the Dock Tower was to stand began.

Above left: *The Palazzo Publico in Siena, Italy, on which Grimsby Dock Tower is modelled.* GUILLAUME BAVIERE*

Above right: *Grimsby Dock Tower: tradition holds that anyone who is born within sight of the tower, whether or not they live in Grimsby, can call themselves a Grimbarian.*

Opposite: *The Dock Tower stands sentinel over Grimsby's harbour, part of which is now this marina.* ROBIN JONES

The tower, which contains a spiral staircase with 39 steps, was designed by James William Wild, and based on the Palazzo Publico in Siena, Italy, which dates from 1297. A classic example of Italian medieval architecture, it was built to house the government of the day. A sister building to the Dock Tower is the clock tower at Birmingham University, which is also based on the Palazzo Publico.

The red bricks from which it was built were baked on site using clay from the Humber bed. It is said that the foundations of the tower were laid on bundles of wool, to absorb sea water which kept inundating the works. The tower was opened by Queen Victoria in October 1854, with Albert ascending to the balcony via the hydraulic lift which once operated inside.

The new Grimsby docks prospered and were expanded to the point where hydraulic power was insufficient. A 78ft electric accumulator tower was built in 1892 next to the Dock Tower and offered nearly nine times as much power.

The Dock Tower became disused as a result, but remained as a much-loved local landmark. The strength of its fabric was tested in 1931 when the town was hit by the Dogger Bank earthquake, which measured 6.1 on the Richter scale and remains the biggest recorded earthquake in Britain. The tower survived unscathed.

It is said that the Dock Tower still managed to perform one of its original intentions, as a navigational aid, during World War Two, but for the wrong reasons.

Luftwaffe bombers heading over the town towards the industrial conurbation of the north like Manchester and Liverpool were thought to have used the Dock Tower as a navigational aid.

Although Grimsby was bombed in several air raids, with 197 fatalities, it is thought that the port got off lightly by comparison because of its unofficial 'lighthouse'. Also, if the Nazis had invaded, Grimsby would have been one of the first landing points in the north of England, as its infrastructure would have still been largely intact, it was later discovered.

The Dock Tower is today a Grade I listed building, but public access is denied by owner Associated British Ports. Grimsby Rotary Club is permitted to hold group climbs up the stairs to the balcony to raise money for charity, with sweeping views across the sea and countryside inland on offer. There have also been charity abseiling stunts, and on 27 June 2012, a torch bearer carrying the Olympic flame abseiled down the tower.

A Lego model of the Dock Tower can be seen at Legoland in Windsor.

Above: *A modern conventional lighthouse, but miniature and purely ornamental, in the sea front gardens at adjacent Cleethorpes.* ROBIN JONES

Right: *Grimsby Dock Tower's sister building, the Birmingham University clock tower.* JO-H*

CHAPTER FOUR
THE HUMBER FORTS

TWO MANMADE ISLANDS, each comprising a fortress, were built during World War One to guard the entrance to the Humber, and have since doubled up as lighthouses.

Haile Sand Fort lies on the low water mark between Cleethorpes and Humberston on the Lincolnshire coast, while Bull Fort rests on a sandbank in the middle of the river.

They were part of a defensive chain which also included fortifications and a military railway along Spurn Head, the great moving sandspit that juts out into the estuary on the Yorkshire side, and which has a traditional lighthouse in its own right.

Bull Fort was built with great difficulty as the sandbank on which it rests is 11ft below low water.

It was constructed to a circular design on interlocking steel piles in the form of caissons. Its outer compartments were filled with concrete and the round inner one with sand, the

Haile Sand Fort, off the coast of Cleethorpes. ROBIN JONES

Above left: When built, Bull Fort was hailed as a marvel of engineering. STREETWISE

Above right: The Drugs rehabilitation project to modernise the interior of Bull Fort. STREETWISE

whole being capped with concrete. The individual floors were then added.

The upper part of the fort stands up to 50ft above high water and comprises three floors and a basement floor, with an outer wall of concrete faced with 12in thick armour plating. It accommodated a garrison of 200 men with all the necessary facilities. Fresh water was pumped up from an artesian well below the estuary bed.

The slightly smaller Haile Sand Fort is similar in design. When completed, the Humber forts were hailed as an outstanding triumph of modern engineering.

In 1919, navigational lights were mounted on both forts, in the case of Bull Fort, on top of a square tower, and at Haile Sand Fort, on top of a mast.

The forts were pressed into service again in World War Two and were a constant target for Nazi aircraft and submarines. A net was installed to prevent the enemy submarines accessing Hull or Grimsby.

In 1956 the army left the forts, which were manned by civilians until the early sixties, when the Humber Conservancy Board took over.

At one time, it was suggested that if a quarter of a mile of Spurn Head was eroded away, Bull Fort would be outside the three-mile limit of British territorial waters and could become a duty free haven.

Bull Fort became a navigational aid, with a huge bell on top automatically rung by a gas pressure hammer, although the light became inactive. An automatic tide gauge was installed to inform ships whether there is sufficient clearance to navigate the Humber.

In 1997, the fort was bought by drugs charity Streetwise, with the aim of turning it into a sanctuary where hardened drug addicts can be isolated from their dealers and weaned off – a diametric opposite to a tax-free drinker's paradise.

Streetwise subsequently obtained planning consent to transform the fort into a residential centre providing a free on-demand 30-day detox programme.

The charity said that the project, renamed Island of Hope, would be able to help 240 addicts every month and would be the largest facility of its kind in the world.

Streetwise trustee Philip Ball said: "It may look like Alcatraz but to them it's an island of hope."

RAF helicopters lowered generators onto the fort to power the tools needed to convert the building.

Haile Sand Fort was bought privately in 1991. Its light is still active, with a 69ft focal plane and a red light flashing every five seconds.

Although it too is not open to the public, it is physically possible to walk out to it at low tide from Cleethorpes, but that is not recommended because the tide comes in quickly and can cut walkers off.

All at sea: Bull Fort at the mouth of the Humber. STREETWISE

CHAPTER FIVE
NOCTON HEATH'S INLAND LIGHTHOUSE

"MUCH DRINKING, wenching and banqueting" was exactly what you would expect if you attended an eighteenth-century private gentlemen's society which became known as the Hell-Fire Club.

Mock rituals, pornography and an 'anything goes" attitude were other characteristics of the club founded by illustrious Lincolnshire resident Sir Francis Dashwood, in hot pursuit of the pleasures of sexual freedom, connoisseurship, and paganism.

By contrast, in his public life, Dashwood, who lived at Nocton Hall in the village of Nocton, at one stage became Chancellor of the Exchequer for, or in spite of, his sins. Thankfully for him, there were no tabloid papers as such in those days.

It was also said that the club played host to black masses and devil worship, although there was no evidence to support such claims.

Dashwood's 'secret' society was by no means unique: 'Hell-Fire Club' was the popular name for several similar clubs established all over Britain and Ireland to cater for high-society rakes.

These clubs were rumoured to be the meeting places of "persons of quality" who wished to take part in immoral acts.

Dashwood's critics said that he was incapable of understanding "a bar bill of five figures" despite his club's infamous excessive consumption of alcohol.

As Chancellor, he caused near riots when he raised a tax on cider, making it more expensive for the working classes, and subsequently resigned in 1763.

His particular club was founded in 1752 and became known as the Friars of Mednenham, after he leased Medmenham Abbey on the River Thames, about six miles from his childhood home of West Wycombe.

Dashwood ordered the abbey to be rebuilt by the architect Nicholas Revett in the style of the eighteenth century Gothic revival, and the motto Fait ce que voudras – do what thou wilt – was placed above a doorway in stained glass.

Beneath the abbey, Dashwood had a series of caves carved out from an existing one. They too were decorated with mythological themes, phallic symbols and other items of a sexual nature.

The club, frequented by large numbers of prostitutes or 'guests', outlasted both the wild rumours and a scandal linking a libellous and pornographic book to the club. Its clandestine activities had died down by 1766 when most of the members were either dead or had moved too far away.

Regardless of what went on in those caves, Dashwood proved himself a public benefactor to Lincolnshire with a display of hellfire above rather than below ground – on top of a 92ft tower. For in the heart of the county, he created one of only three true inland lighthouses in Britain.

Several lighthouses in England have been set back from the shore, like Southwold, which stands in the middle of its town, but Dashwood's was 35 miles from the nearest coast!

It stood in the middle of lonely, isolated Dunston Heath to the south of Lincoln, a wild, untamed tract of open windswept countryside that was still desolate and uninhabited in the eighteenth century.

Opposite: *Lofty Dunston Pillar, built by Sir Francis Dashwood, founder of one of the 18th-century Hell-Fire clubs.* ROBIN JONES

Left: *The bust of George III created from the remains of the statue on Dunston Pillar now sits in the grounds of Lincoln Castle.* ROBIN JONES

Below: *The entrance to the staircase.* ROBIN JONES

Travellers making their way from Sleaford to Lincoln lived in fear of being confronted by highwaymen on the heath, an all-too regular occurrence.

One such hold-up ended in the murder of Christopher Wilkinson, who refused to stand and deliver to none other than Dick Turpin. The heath was at the western edge of land owned by Dashwood, who became determined to make the road safer.

He ordered a land lighthouse to be built, similar in design to the central cupola of Nocton Hall, but much higher to ensure that beams of light would spread across extensive brush waste to deter highwaymen.

Travellers would use the tower, which became known as Dunston Pillar, as a beacon to find their way.

Finished in 1751, the pillar had a spiral staircase inside the tower to take the lighthouse keeper to the gallery which surrounded the base of the octagonal 15ft lantern.

The magnificent view from the tower took in Lincoln Cathedral to the north and Boston

The remains of one of the original 1751 inscriptions on the lighthouse. On the east side was inscribed Dunston Pillar, the north side 'To Lincoln V Miles', the south side: 'From the City CXX Miles' and on the west side 'Columnam Hane Utilitate Publicae, DDD F Dashwood, MDCCLI.'
ROBIN JONES

William Hogarth's 1750s painting Sir Francis Dashwood at his Devotions. The artist parodies Renaissance images showing St Francis of Assisi at prayer. By contrast, Dashwood is portrayed staring devotedly at the mirage of a naked woman lying seductively.

Stump to the far southeast.

Not only did it do its job as a navigational aid as intended, being regularly lit until 1788, but took off as a tourist attraction in its own right. Assembly rooms, a bowling green and picnic area where travellers could rest and pass the time sprang up at its foot.

Eventually, the heath was tamed and became good arable land with a turnpike road – now the A15 – crossing it, and as the population increased, the highwaymen faded away.

The lantern gradually collapsed as the ironwork rusted and, in 1808, was destroyed in a storm, rendering the lighthouse useless.

Two years later, the lantern was replaced with a statue of King George III by the Earl of Buckinghamshire to celebrate the monarch's Golden Jubilee.

The 15ft tall statue was built of a unique material called coade stone, which had been invented in 1769 by Eleanor Coade (1733-1821). It was a moulded artificial stone material with a hard surface finish, like a ceramic, that had to be subjected to a vast amount of heat for several days in a kiln. The pre-moulded statue was hollow inside and held together with iron bolts encased in lead to prevent rust from affecting the stone. Unfortunately the mason, John Wilson, aged 56, of nearby Harmston, fell to his death whilst erecting it on 9 September 1810.

He is now buried in the village graveyard at Harmston with his gravestone featuring a relief carving of the Pillar and the inscription in both English and Latin "He who erected the noble King, here now laid by Deaths sharp sting" and "Qui erexit nobilem Regem, Nune hic jacet per Mortis legen."

A nineteenth-century engraving of Dunston Pillar topped with the statue.
ILLUSTRATED LONDON NEWS

In 1941, Dunston Pillar was deemed a hazard to low-flying aircraft approaching nearby RAF Waddington and Coleby Heath, and was therefore lowered by 60ft to remove the risk of a crash. The statue of King George III was literally kicked off the top of the tower and smashed to pieces on the ground below.

However, the pieces were saved and stored, and most of the fragments are now in the possession of Lincolnshire County Council in the cellars of the old prison in Lincoln Castle where they can be viewed today.

Eventually, the head and shoulders of the statue were reconstructed by local monumental mason John Ivory as a bust in its own right and placed on display in the grounds of Lincoln Castle where it stands now. The Heritage Trust of Lincolnshire would like to see the original, full-length statue rebuilt to its former glory, but the estimated £300,000 cost has so far proved a stumbling block.

In 1991, Dunston had a wooden replica of the statue and pillar commissioned for the grounds of the village hall.

The remainder of the tower is still a well-known landmark, albeit surrounded by trees and hedges which would not have been there in 1751, and a public footpath passes close by.

While the scandalous stories about devil worship were probably untrue, hell fire eventually did descend on Dashwood's home.

The hall, constructed in the 1670s from a manor house built from the remains of Norman priory buildings on the site, burned down in 1834.

Rebuilt in 1841 for the first Earl of Ripon, the site also accommodated the US Army's 7th General Hospital during World War Two.

A Grade II listed building, the hall burned down again on 24 October 2004, and was left as a shell, although its structural integrity remained.

In October 2009, it was listed by the Victorian Society amongst the top 10 endangered buildings list in England and Wales, and the owners are looking at ways of restoring it.

This modern wooden interpretation of the statue of George III on Dunston Pillar stands in front of Dunston's village hall two miles to the east. The Dashwood family also owned the village. ROBIN JONES

CHAPTER SIX
BOSTON STUMP

THE DEFINING LANDMARK of the south Lincolnshire coast has to be Boston Stump.

The 272ft tower of one of the biggest parish churches in England, correctly known as Saint Botolph's parochial church of Boston, on a clear day can be seen from the Norfolk side of The Wash, towering above the surrounding flat fenland.

In historic times, its height rendered it eminently suitable for use as a lighthouse.

Legend has it that the church was built on the site of a monastery founded by St Botolph in 654. It is known that a small Norman church existed there, and was replaced by a far larger structure to reflect Boston's huge importance by the start of the fourteenth century. By then its trade rivalled that of London and it also had four monasteries.

The existing church was begun in 1309 under Sir John Truesdale, the vicar of St Botolph's, and was completed around 1390. Because it was built so close to the tidal River Witham just 33ft away, there were problems with the foundations and so the chancel was extended to prop the building up and create greater structural stability, as the nave piers were leaning dangerously to the east.

The perpendicular tower was not started until 1450, and because of the earlier design of the foundations, it leans by less than half a centimetre despite its great height – a magnificent feat of medieval engineering. It was completed by 1502.

The tower became used as a marker both for travellers on the Fens and seafarers in The Wash.

It is believed that a lantern was lit inside the tower as a "sea-mark", and there were rings from which it was hung via a pulley.

In 1612, the church was damaged by militant local puritans, and later that century, vicar John Cotton preached from the grand pulpit installed that year which reflected the perceived importance of preaching in those times. In 1633, Cotton moved to Massachusetts following the earlier settlement by the Pilgrim Fathers, who had sailed from Boston via Plymouth. Cotton played a major role in the founding and naming of Boston, Massachusetts.

The Roundhead forces which occupied the church during the English Civil War destroyed many of its windows, but major restoration was carried out during 1851-53.

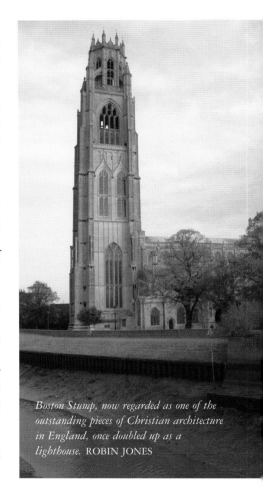

Boston Stump, now regarded as one of the outstanding pieces of Christian architecture in England, once doubled up as a lighthouse. ROBIN JONES

Looking up inside the tower of St Botolph's church. ROBIN JONES

During World War Two, the tower again became a navigational aid – for both sides. Lincolnshire's huge number of front-line airbases earned it the name 'Bomber County' and both British and US pilots used the Stump as a guide to return home. The Luftwaffe also used it as a marker, and by comparison with other ports, Boston experienced few air raids.

When floodlighting was installed at the Stump in the twenty-first century, the yellow lighting of the octagonal lantern was specially installed to represent its use as a medieval navigational marker.

The village of Leverton to the north of Boston, which had a harbour or haven known as the Ostrich until it silted up several centuries ago, may have had a lighthouse. An account of 1814 stated that the remains of a lighthouse were to be found on a hill above the salt marshes near Hurn End.

Below left: An early twentieth-century view of Boston Stump on the bank of the River Witham. ROBIN JONES COLLECTION

Below right: In 1971, the Inner Dowsing lightship in the North Sea, helping to guard sea lanes to Boston as well as along the east coast, was replaced after a century by a former National Coal Board drilling rig standing 14 miles off the coast of Skegness. The light tower's lantern stood 142ft above the sea. COURTESY EASTERN DAILY PRESS

CHAPTER SEVEN
THE NENE TWINS

The East Bank lighthouse, which once stood three miles out into the middle of tidal salt marshes. ROBIN JONES

THE PAIR OF LIGHTHOUSES which stand sentinel near the entrance to the River Nene north of Sutton Bridge date from 1830. They were built to commemorate the draining of the Great Fens and the mouth of the River Nene following its diversion as part of the land reclamation project.

In 1827, an Act of Parliament was passed allowing a new channel to be cut and land to be reclaimed on this part of the Lincolnshire fens, notorious as the district where bad King John lost his treasure baggage train to the quicksands a few days before his death. Two years later, another Act permitted the erection of two lighthouses, or beacons, at the seaward end of the new cut, to guide shipping to the ports of Sutton Bridge and Wisbech.

The pair were necessary because the cut entered deep water at a point where the Nene estuary was three miles wide, at the southern end of The Wash. It was feared that ships could easily miss the entrance to the river, even in daylight.

The architect of the lighthouses, which are similar in shape to small windmills, was John Rennie the Younger, the son of canal and dock builder John Rennie.

The younger Rennie's first major job was overseeing the laying of the foundations of Waterloo Bridge in 1813. Two years later he helped his father build Southwark Bridge, and then, along with Philip Richards, designed the Royal William Victualling Yard in Plymouth.

His greatest achievement, however, was the building of London Bridge, for which his father who died in 1821 had drawn plans.

The bridge was opened in 1831, after which he was knighted.

In Lincolnshire, he was responsible for the New River Ancholme drainage scheme in the north of the county, and with Thomas Telford, the Nene outfall at Wisbech, which was completed in 1831, a year after the East and West lighthouses.

He became president of the Institution of Civil Engineers on 25 June 1844.

The lighthouses were merely daymarks, because although they look the part, they did not have lights. When built, the western lighthouse lay only a short distance from dry land, but the eastern lighthouse was at the end of a three-mile embankment running into the middle of

The West Bank lighthouse is a private house. ROBIN JONES

The twin Nene lighthouses, the East Bank on the left and the West Bank in the foreground on the right, separated by the manmade channel that takes the River Nene into The Wash. ROBIN JONES

the tidal marshes, with the new Nene cut on one side and the sands of the old Nene estuary on the other.

The lighthouses are 55ft tall and stand about 15ft above high water. They can be seen by shipping 20 miles away. The East lighthouse also served as a customs hailing station. As ships came in with the tide, customs officials would hail them through a megaphone to ask what goods were on board and what was their destination.

The lighthouses become home to either employees of the River Nene authorities or families linked to local farming communities.

However, in 1933, the then rundown and damp East Bank lighthouse became home to 24-year-old Peter Markham Scott, who rented it from the Nene Catchment Board for £5 a year. He had been trying to rent it for several years, having first discovered it in December 1929 while on a wildfowling expedition with two friends in a new punt he had bought in Cambridge, and which was named *Kazarka*, Russian for the red-breasted goose,

Born on 14 September 1909, Peter's father – the great Antarctic explorer Robert Falcon Scott – perished when he was just two, after failing in his expedition to become the first to reach the South Pole.

In a final letter to his wife, sculptor Kathleen Bruce, Scott told her to "make the boy interested in natural history if you can; it is better than games."

Peter Scott graduated from Trinity College, Cambridge, in History of Art in 1931. He held his first art exhibition in London two years later.

Money from the proceeds of the exhibit were used by Peter to restore the rundown lighthouse from where he enjoyed perfect views of wading birds. He built a studio, bedroom, and new garages.

He was never alone at the lighthouse. The local coastguard used what later became the kitchen and an old man called Charlie, who collected mussels and camphor to eke out a living, inhabited the basement. It was also still in use as a customs hailing post.

While he lived at the lighthouse, Peter developed his writing and painting to widespread acclaim.

The wildfowl inspired Scott's first book, *Morning Flight*, which contains many paintings completed at the lighthouse.

Peter eventually became one of the world's foremost figures in nature and conservation and was knighted in 1973 for his many achievements.

He became a founder member of the World Wildlife Fund (now the World Wide Fund for Nature) and the Wildfowl and Wetlands Trust based at Slimbridge in Gloucestershire.

He left his mark on the lighthouse in the form of an etching of 12 mallards on what had been the outside wall of the lighthouse, accompanied by the words 'November 1937, Peter Scott'.

His friend, American writer Paul Gallico, visited Peter at the lighthouse and was inspired

A blue plaque on East Bank lighthouse remembering Sir Peter Scott's occupancy. ROBIN JONES

Opposite: *Sir Peter Scott and a flock of his geese at East Bank lighthouse in the Thirties.* COURTESY EASTERN DAILY PRESS

Wildfowl swoop over the grounds of East Bank lighthouse, almost in memory of Sir Peter Scott! ROBIN JONES

to write the romantic wildlife fiction classic *The Snow Goose*. In it, he moved the lighthouse 70 miles south to a fictional spot to place the hero within sailing distance of the Dunkirk beaches, but it was clear that the inspiration was East Bank. The fictional lighthouse was described as "Desolate, utterly lonely and made lonelier by the calls and cries of the wildfowl that make their homes in the marshlands and saltings." Peter painted many of the illustrations for the novel, and they are clearly based on his own photographs of East Bank.

Peter represented Great Britain and Northern Ireland at sailing in the 1936 Olympic Games in Berlin, winning a bronze medal.

However, three years later he went off to fight Nazi Germany, enlisting in the Royal Navy, and earning the Distinguished Service Cross for bravery.

The army requisitioned the lighthouse and made plans to cut off the top floor and use it as a gun platform, but these were dropped after protests from Peter's mother.

It is said that he did not return to live at the lighthouse after the war.

While he lived there in the thirties, the tides still came right up to it. By the end of the war, there was a desperate need for more farmland to feed a ration book nation, and the sea walls had been extended a further half mile out to reclaim more of the salt marsh. The two lighthouses that used to mark the entrance to the River Nene were left isolated among the cornfields that eventually came.

Also, the nearby mudflats had become a bombing range, shattering the peace and quiet.

Realising he could no longer keep his flocks of wildfowl on tidal pools and saltings next to the lighthouse, Peter sadly gave it up.

It was then leased as a holiday home by a Mr Gandy, a baker and industrialist, who rendered the tower, protecting the porous brickwork.

When he died in the Sixties, the Fenland Wildfowlers leased the lighthouse for ten years as their headquarters and accommodation for their marsh warden.

The group abandoned it after a dispute over maintenance costs. The lighthouse passed into the ownership of Anglian Water and, badly vandalised, stood empty for years.

It was all but a ruin when in 1985 it was bought by a friend and admirer of Peter, Royal Navy Commander David Joel. Not only did he restore the lighthouse, preserving as much original fabric as possible, but he created ponds on the site of Peter's first wildfowl pools and stocked them with many species including snow geese.

Electricity was connected for the first time, and plumbing was installed.

Commander Joel spent around £250,000 on the property.

He even kept the lamps in the tower burning at night on a voluntary basis, as did the private owner of the West Bank lighthouse, to help bait diggers who got lost in the fog.

In late 2010, the lighthouse, now Grade II* listed, was sold to conservationists, Doug and Sue Hilton, who had developed a 65-acre nature reserve, Buckland Lake, in disused chalkpits at Cliffe in Kent.

A 2009 edition of Paul Gallico's wildlife classic The Snow Goose.

Sir John Rennie, who built the Nene lighthouses and co-engineered the Nene outfall.

They changed the name of their organisation to the Snowgoose Wildlife Trust, to honour the lighthouse's great literary legacy, and obtained planning permission to turn the lighthouse into a visitor centre.

Their plans include a museum dedicated to Peter's life and achievements to be set up in the garages that he built and a Sir Peter Scott Millennium Centre visitor centre, to be constructed in the grounds. It is hoped that it will become a major visitor destination for international conservationists who will be once again able to walk in the landscape that inspired Peter, who died in 1989, who did so much to protect the global natural habitat.

A public footpath called the St Peter Scott Walk runs along the east bank of the Nene. The West Bank lighthouse, which is almost identical, is a private house, with several recent additions including a conservatory, and a small customs jetty below. It is Grade II listed. A public footpath along the west bank runs past.

The gateway to Sir Peter Scott's former lighthouse home. ROBIN JONES

The West Bank lighthouse is nowadays all but encased by tree foliage in the summer months. ROBIN JONES

CHAPTER EIGHT
OLD HUNSTANTON

IT IS A TRICK PUB QUIZ question to ask from which part of the East Anglia coast can you see the sun set. The answer is the east coastline of The Wash, the great eternal swish of waters between the silt-laden Fenland rivers that empty into it and the North Sea which brings in deposits of sand and shingle.

Somewhat akin to the Zuiderzee in The Netherlands, but with no realistic chance of similar reclamation, The Wash is an 18-mile-wide sea within a sea.

It has always been possible to navigate the deep channels which have formed between the great sandbanks from north to south, leading to ports like Boston, Wisbech and King's Lynn, but navigation aids are a must.

The distinctive feature of Hunstanton is the stripy orange and white cliffs that rear up north of the resort, and on which the original settlement of Old Hunstanton sits. These are the only cliffs on a short otherwise comprising saltmarsh, mudflats, shingle and, at the northern end, some sand, and their height makes them eminently suitable for positioning navigation markers or lights.

The first such sea mark was a chapel built in 1272 on top of St Edmund's Point, recalling the 14-year-old Saxon king and martyr said to have landed here in 855AD to lay claim to East Anglia. He was killed by the Danes after refusing to renounce his Christianity.

A hermit may have lived in the chapel, and the light from his windows on the clifftops was said to have helped seamen find their bearings.

All around Britain, early marker lights were provided by churches, chapels and monasteries, and became known as ecclesiastical lights. Boston Stump was a classic example. Often these came about by accident rather than deliberation.

Hunstanton's first light became known as the Chapel Light, a name that persisted even after a purpose-built conventional lighthouse was built. A later hermit named John Puttock constructed a 100ft beacon on the cliffs, according to one account.

As King's Lynn and Boston prospered greatly in the fifteenth and sixteenth centuries, a group of merchants from the former drew up plans in 1663 for erecting a permanent lighthouse at the entrance to The Wash. There was only one section of high ground available, and so that was the obvious choice for a site. A petition was presented to Charles II on 1

The old lighthouse on Hunstanton's cliffs. ROBIN JONES

August that year, and it was referred to Trinity House in London, which gave its approval, with a stipulation that vessels passing on the northern coast should not be forced to pay for its upkeep if they did not use the two ports.

John Knight, a staunch royalist who had acted as surgeon to the forces of Charles I in the English Civil War, obtained from Charles II permission to build a lighthouse on the cliffs and charge tolls to passing ships.

By the time final approval was signed by the king on 3 June 1665, two towers had already been built, and they were lit for the first time that October. The following February, Knight signed over the rights to the light to wealthy Lynn merchant Edward Bodham, who was married to his half-sister Frances, and who had been backing the scheme clandestinely all along, knowing he would not have stood the same chance of winning the king's approval in his own right.

An early twentieth-century postcard view of Hunstanton lighthouse in its operational days. ROBIN JONES COLLECTION

Illumination was provided by a coal-fired light at the top of the wooden towers, and a front light comprising candles. It may have been that the light was enclosed inside a lantern, oxygen being supplied to the fire by bellows, a revolutionary move in its day. Elsewhere, the first recorded case of an enclosed fire light is at Lowestoft in 1677.

The lighthouse burned down in late 1777, and was replaced by a 33ft circular wooden tower.

History was then made at Hunstanton. Alderman Edward Everard, who then held the rights to the light, approached King's Lynn-based physicist Ezekial Walker who had written several papers on optics and illumination.

Walker agreed to provide illumination for the new lighthouse, and studied developments on Merseyside where lighthouses at Hoylake and Bidston Hill had been fitted with large wooden reflectors lined with silvered glass.

Walker took this technology, which had been invented by William Hutchinson, to the next stage, and installed 18 smaller mirror reflectors instead of a single large one.

Opposite: *Hunstanton lighthouse as framed by the ruins of its predecessor, St Edmund's Chapel.* ROBIN JONES

A plaque staking the lighthouse's claim to have had the world's first parabolic reflector. ROBIN JONES

The 1907-built disused coastguard lookout next to the lighthouse on the cliffs. A plaque records that it was visited on April 24 1943 by George VI, Queen Elizabeth, and the princesses Elizabeth and Margaret. It has also served as a Marconi listening station and during World War One successfully plotted the location of the German fleet prior to the Battle of Jutland. ROBIN JONES

Each of the reflectors, made of copper coated with silver, was shaped into the form of a parabolic curve. An oil lamp was fixed in the exact centre, where the light rays would be concentrated to maximum intensity. It was the world's first parabolic reflector.

Parabolic reflectors are used to collect energy from a distant source and bring it to a common focal point, thus correcting the aberration of simpler spherical reflectors. Since the principles of reflection are reversible, parabolic reflectors can also be used to project energy of a source at its focus outward in a parallel beam, and are used in car headlights, for example. There is a debate as to whether it was invented by Hutchinson, as evident at Bidston Hill, or Walker, who improved the technology.

When it was lit for the first time in 1778, the Hunstanton lighthouse literally outshone all others, and so Walker had changed the course of lighthouse technology. It was also one of the first lighthouses to be lit by oil rather than a brazier of coal.

It was nine years before the idea was taken up elsewhere, but parabolic reflectors gradually became standard features in lighthouses everywhere.

Despite this innovation, Everard's tower was becoming outdated, and in the first decades of the nineteenth century, many complaints about the light were made by seamen.

In February 1826, after the government began looking seriously at taking over the remaining private lighthouses on Britain's shores, then owner Samuel Lane backtracked on an earlier reluctance to sell it to Trinity House, but wanted too much money. Instead, in 1832, he installed new reflectors.

In 1836, Parliament finally gave Trinity House approval to take over the private lighthouses the following year. In 1838, Trinity House began work on a new 61ft brick tower, with a lantern containing Argand lamps and polished reflectors. A light was shone for the first time on 3 September 1840.

It showed a fixed white light, but followed the previous practice of red reflectors facing the Roaring Middle Sand. The lantern was 12ft in diameter, while the light was 49ft from the base of the tower and around 110ft above sea level.

By this time, Hunstanton's lighthouse was not the only sea mark in The Wash. In 1828, Trinity House moored a lightship at the head of the Long Sand in the mouth of the great inlet, and named it Lynn Well. In 1872, another was moored by King's Lynn Corporation at Bar Flat, where the channels leading to the three ports enter the sea, and was moved in 1907 to a position beyond Roaring Middle.

A series of six lightships along the North Sea coast between Humber and Norfolk

FIRE OVER ENGLAND
THIS BEACON WAS ONE
OF 400 LIT AROUND
GREAT BRITAIN
ON 19 JULY 1988
TO CELEBRATE THE
400 ANNIVERSARY OF
THE SIGHTING OF
THE GREAT SPANISH
ARMADA OF 1588

This coal-fired brazier near the lighthouse and reminiscent of an early lighthouse fire basket recalls the lighting of beacons across Britain to warn of the arrival of the Spanish Armada in 1588. ROBIN JONES

including Lynn Well rendered the land lighthouse redundant, although World War One gave it a stay of execution when it became a naval wireless station. The last light was shone from Hunstanton lighthouse on 29 September 1921, and the following January, it was sold by auction along with its contents, the lantern house being subsequently removed and replaced with a single storey structure. The building was bought by the Le Strange Estate.

The buildings became a dwelling and a tea room for holidaymakers, but the tower decayed through lack of use. It was commandeered as a military observation post during World War Two and then sold on again. In 1965, the local council sold it off for conversion to a private home.

In 2007, owner Bip Weatherall, a member of the sixties rock band the Tornadoes, famous for their hit Telstar, offered the Grade II listed structure for sale. Now marketed by its new owner as the Old Lighthouse, it was fully restored and converted to four-bedroom holiday accommodation in 1997. Next to the lighthouse stand the ruins of its predecessor, St Edmund's Chapel.

The Lynn Well lightship outlived the land light.

Many of the Trinity House lightships were stationed around the east coast of England, where shoals extend well out to sea and where there is much coastal trade. Indeed, the first light vessel was anchored at the Nore, the entrance to the Thames, in 1732.

Lightships were made of wood until 1886, after which they were iron, and from 1936 all were of steel construction. Unpowered, they were towed into position to drop anchor.

The crews comprised two masters and nine ratings, with one master and up to six ratings aboard at one time. The Lynn Well lightship had four ratings: three lightmen first class and one lightman third class. Each master served four weeks afloat and four ashore, while the ratings served four aboard with a fortnight ashore.

Victuals were taken out once every two weeks from Great Yarmouth, along with fuel for the light.

Popular pleasure steam boat trips from Skegness pier to the Lynn Well lightship were run from 1882. Also in the 1850s and '60s, the annual Lynn Roads regatta took place with sailing boats racing on a 40-mile course around the lightship.

In the 1950s, local newspaper the *Lynn News and Advertiser* successfully appealed for readers to donate money to buy a TV set for the crew.

The cost of maintaining manpower-intensive lightships was expensive, so Trinity House drew up plans to replace them with automatic buoys.

Lynn Well lightship and her fog siren were replaced by a navigation buoy, a LANBY (large automatic navigation buoy) in 1973. The last lightship moored there, LV89, was sold and became a sea cadets training ship in Norwich for several years. She was later used as a pub in Bristol before being broken up in 1995.

CHAPTER NINE
EAST DUDGEON LIGHTSHIP

BRITISH PRIME MINISTER Neville Chamberlain is best remembered for waving a piece of paper and uttering the phrase "peace in our time."

When the likes of maverick Conservative politicians such as Winston Churchill had pessimistically maintained that there could be no lasting peace with Nazi Germany, Chamberlain had been party to the Munich agreement of 1938 which saw the partition of Czechoslovakia.

Clouds had been gradually darkening on the horizon, but there were those who saw that appeasement was the best if not the only way of avoiding another bloodbath like the Great War.

It was Chamberlain, however, who broadcast to the nation on 3 September 1940, informing the nation that following the invasion of Poland, Britain was now at war with Germany.

Any lingering doubt must surely have vanished when on 8 February 1940, the Prime Minister addressed the packed House of Commons, and spoke about the brutality of the Hitler regime in the countries it strove to oppress, and described in detail a Luftwaffe attack on a defenceless lightship off the Norfolk coast on the morning of Monday 29 January.

Lightships had for centuries been treated as neutral during wartime, helping all shipping irrespective of its ownership by a friendly or a hostile power.

The ill-fated East Dudgeon lightship.
BELTON & DISTRICT HISTORICAL
SOCIETY

History records, however, that the Nazi regime did not do decency. That basic fact was rammed home by the attack on the East Dudgeon lightship off Cromer, which left seven of its eight-man crew dead.

Up to then, the pilots of passing German aircraft had waved to the crew, who waved back. It was somewhat reminiscent of British and German troops sharing Christmas cheer in the trenches in World War One, but on a permanent basis.

The crew was therefore shocked to see a Heinkel aircraft coming from the direction of the English coast around 9.30am diving to attack, machine-gunning the decks to ensure that there could be no resistance.

The Heinkel turned around and came back for a second attack, this time dropping nine

John Sanders, the sole survivor of the cowardly attack on the lightship. BELTON & DISTRICT HISTORICAL SOCIETY

A snapshot of the East Dudgeon lightship crew in 1932. BELTON & DISTRICT HISTORICAL SOCIETY

Opposite: *A subsequent lighthouse that served at Dudgeon, as well as other East Anglian stations including Owers, Smith's Knoll, Shipwash and Cross Sand. Built in 1944/45 for Trinity House, she was based at Dudgeon from September 1974 until January 1975. Decommissioned in 1993, she was sold to Dean & Reddyhoff Ltd., Southampton, for use as a marina clubhouse at Gosport in Hampshire. She was substantially modified and painted green, and renamed* Mary Mouse *after directors' wives Mary Deddyhoff and Joanna (Mouse) Dean.*

bombs on the lightship, No. 62, one of a series built in the 1890s. The last scored a direct hit.

One of two boats was destroyed, but the crew, including one member who had been ill in his bunk, managed to get into the other. The Heinkel did not strike again, and the crew began rowing towards the shore, which they almost reached around 2am the following day after a marathon 17-hour struggle.

With waves breaking on the shore, they dropped anchor, and then the boat capsized.

Only one crew member made it to dry land, John Sanders, aged 31, of Great Yarmouth. Rather than try to swim for it, he lay on his back in the icy water, exhausted. "I had heard one of my mates shouting as the waves carried him ahead of me, but in the darkness I could not find any of them," he said.

Eventually, he drifted into calmer water, and after managing to regain some strength, crawled ashore. The bodies of his shipmates were later found washed up.

The Heinkel had earlier taken part in heavy German air raids that took place over the 400 miles of the British coastline between Kent and the Tay lasting between 9am on the 29th and noon the following day.

No longer under any illusion about peace, Chamberlain, soon to be replaced by Churchill, told the Commons: "Attacks by German aeroplanes on British and neutral ships, which have recently increased in intensity, are claimed by the enemy as great victories in the war against British shipping. These raids are generally carried out on days when low thick clouds cover the shipping lanes."

He continued: "The extent of the successes claimed by Germany for this method of attack bears no relation to the facts. For example, on 3rd February it was asserted by the enemy that in the air raid on that day along the East Coast, no less than nine merchantmen, as well as other vessels, were sunk, and that the British ships sunk were all in convoy. The facts are that, in this raid, one Norwegian merchantman was sunk and no British merchant ship was lost.

"These vauntings are poured out like a smoke screen to conceal stories of callous brutality as inhuman as any yet recorded of the enemy. The bombing of unarmed merchant ships and fishing boats from the air, followed by machine gunning of the crews at elevations which make it quite clear that there could be no doubt as to their identity, are now all too familiar.

"The German wireless statement on 30th of last month that 'The British Naval Patrol Vessel East Dudgeon has been sunk by German aircraft' is a falsification intended to cover up from the world a deliberate and savage attack on a lightship.

"To seafaring folks of all nations the 'East Dudgeon' is well known as a lightship, and its identity was unmistakable. She was, naturally, unarmed. We have always shared, with other civilised nations, the view that lightships because of the nature of their services are outside the scope of hostilities, and, in the case of British lightships, they are not even utilised to report the presence of enemy craft in their vicinity.

"On the morning of the 30th an enemy aeroplane was seen totally over the 'East Dudgeon' lightship. The only survivor of the crew of eight tells his story simply in these words: We were not alarmed because on previous occasions German pilots had waved to us and left us alone. But on this occasion the bomber dived suddenly and sprayed the deck with machine-gun bullets, and later dropped nine bombs, the last of which hit our ship. That is briefly the story of the attack on the lightship 'East Dudgeon.'

"The dead bodies of seven of her defenceless crew were found next morning on the sea shore. The killing of fishermen, merchant seamen, and of lightship crews in circumstances such as I have related, is not war but murder. Such acts of pure gangsterism can have little, if any, practical effect on the outcome of the war.

"The horror and disgust which they excite in the minds of all decent peoples only make us the more resolved to carry on the struggle until civilisation is purged of such wickedness."

Another light vessel based at Dudgeon was LV11, constructed by renowned lightship builder Philip & Son of Dartmouth in 1951. First stationed at Dudgeon, she broke free from her moorings on 1 February 1953. Afterwards she served at Morecambe Bay, St Gowan and Bar stations. She was withdrawn on 21 October 1988 and later rebuilt as a floating restaurant in The Netherlands, although the light was left in working order. After changes of ownership she was towed from Rotterdam to Krimpen in April 2009 to continue in this role at a new location. QUISTNIX*

History records that the bestiality of the Nazis did not improve.

The incident formed the basis of a 1940 British propaganda film, *The Men of the Lightship*, made by the Scottish-born Hollywood-trained director David MacDonald.

Premiered in three large London theatres, it highlighted British courage in a moving account of the bombing of the lightship, with pre-war censorship thrown to the winds. During the attack on the lightship a gnarled seaman crouching on the open deck looks up at the Heinkel raking the ship with machine gun fire and remarks "the dirty bastards."

To prevent such a tragedy happening again, some lightships were withdrawn from their stations by Trinity House, creating a navigational problem for shipping. However, they were gradually reinstated, but armed with one anti-aircraft gun each.

Another wartime casualty was the Newarp lightship, eight miles off Great Yarmouth. Here, two lightships, unmanned to prevent more casualties in Luftwaffe attacks, and one light float were sunk during the war.

The Dudgeon station was the world's second lightship, the first being a lightvessel placed by inventor David Avery at the Nore at the entrance to the Thames in 1731, despite opposition from Trinity House who thought the idea was of little merit. Avery's partner was former King's Lynn barber and ship manager Robert Hamblin.

After the Nore lightvessel was shown to be a great success, Trinity House acquired the patent, following which, the Dudgeon lightship was placed in position in 1736, with others at Owers in 1748 and Newarp in 1790.

The lightship station at Dudgeon was decommissioned in 1988.

In 2013, with the opening by Warwick Energy of a new 100-turbine wind farm 18 miles off Cromer at Dudgeon, new shipping and navigation aids will be installed. The wind turbines will be painted, marked and fitted with navigation lights in accordance with statutory requirements.

Another calamity that befell a lightship from the North Norfolk coast took place in August 1967, when LV83 was being towed from Outer Sands station to South Shields for a refit. Despite the fact a red-painted lightship is fairly unmistakeable, the Polish trawler *Snardy* rammed her at speed.

The startled lightship crew were woken by the impact of the collision and jumped down from their bunks to find themselves waist deep in water, They could not get out to the deck, but at the last moment managed to open a small hatch and struggled through to the open air. They had just enough time to jump into a lifeboat sent back from their tug before the lightship sank.

Rediscovered by a salvage diver 14 miles off Easington, Cleveland, in the 1980s, it is now a destination for diving expeditions.

CHAPTER TEN
THE CROMER QUARTET

A PRIMARY REASON for the predominance of lightships like East Dudgeon around the coast of East Anglia was the coal trade from Newcastle to London.

The collier fleets hugged the calmer waters between the coast and the North Sea sandbanks, but between Flamborough Head and Yarmouth Roads, they had to sail out into the open sea, losing sight of land. When they passed Norfolk, it was time to move inshore again.

Cromer lighthouse is built safely back from the sea. ROBIN JONES

A high light was needed with sufficient visibility to be seen so far away, and the perfect place was the clay cliffs of Cromer.

Here, the sea is forever taking away cliff debris, causing the coastline to recede inland. The early medieval settlement of Shipden was lost to the waves, leaving, for the time being, the lofty headland of Foulness Point, surrounded on three sides by sea.

In 1549, it was designated as a beacon site, used to sound the alarm across the country in times of national crisis.

The first illuminated seamark, however, in these parts, is said to be an ecclesiastical light shone from the top of the Cromer parish church of St Peter & St Paul, which would have been of benefit only to local shipping.

Following the demise of Shipden, Edward III granted permission in 1337 for a replacement church at Cromer. It was built in what is now the middle of the town between 1377 and 1437. Perpendicular in style, at 160ft it boasts the highest tower in Norfolk. It fell into decay in the seventeenth and eighteenth centuries and was restored in 1885.

Much more was needed than a candle lit in a church window to make the coastline safe for bigger shipping, a fact not lost on Middlesex speculator Sir John Clayton who, together with a George Blake, in 1669 petitioned Charles II for permission to build four lighthouses on the east coast, including one at Foulness Point, and another at St Nicholas Gat opposite Corton near Lowestoft and Great Yarmouth.

London Trinity House opposed the bid, in order to safeguard its ancient rights of controlling navigational aids, and despite Charles II signing letters patent for the lighthouses on 25 October that year, the legal battle against Clayton and Blake continued.

In 1674, Clayton leased a parcel of land on Foulness Point to build a lighthouse, which was achieved within two years, but it was not lit. However, further protests from Trinity House led to Clayton's supporter Charles II bowing to pressure and referring the dispute to the Committee for Trade and Plantations for an inquiry.

Meanwhile, Trinity House campaigned for shipmasters not to pay any fees to him for his light.

Eventually, thwarted by the continual legal objections, he surrendered the patent for his lighthouses apart from the one at Corton, the only one to be lit. His tower at Foulness Point, meanwhile, was marked on Admiralty charts as "a lighthouse but no fire kept in", unlit but serving some use as a marker. It was sent crashing into the sea by cliff erosion around 1700.

Trinity House turned deaf ears to pleas for a seamark at Cromer for the next four decades, but in 1718, Ipswich merchant Edward Bowell raised a petition for a lighthouse at Foulness Point, and Trinity House agreed to let him build it at his own expense while paying £100 a year in rent on a 61-year lease from the day of the first light being shone.

Bowell's partner in the scheme was Nathaniel Life, who owned the site of the proposed tower, and who had himself become concerned at the loss of the daymark with the demise of

A stained glass window in Cromer parish church recalls Edward Bowell's lighthouse which fell into the sea in 1866. ROBIN JONES

Opposite: *The former lighthouse keepers' cottages at Cromer.* ROBIN JONES

Above left: *The tower of Cromer parish church from which early lights were shone for local seafarers.*
ROBIN JONES

Above right: *The only Clayton lighthouse to survive is the chalk tower at Flamborough Head in Yorkshire, but it never shone a light.*
ADAM WYLES*

Clayton's tower.

A coal fire providing the illuminations from the new brick tower was first lit on 29 September 1719, the year the tower was built. It was enclosed in a lantern rather than contained in an open brazier.

When the lease ended in 1780, Trinity House extended it to Bowell's nephew Thomas Bowell by 42 years.

A severe storm which caused numerous shipwrecks along the coast of East Anglia on 31 October 1789 prompted Trinity House to demand upgrades to lighthouses, and the Foulness lighthouse followed in the footsteps of Hunstanton 12 years earlier by being converted to oil burning.

It was also fitted with a second flashing light, five reflectors and Argand oil fired lamps on three sides of a revolving frame, which rotated when pulled by a descending weight.

Swiss physicist and chemist François Pierre Ami Argand (5 July 1750 – 14 October 1803, invented a cylindrical wick lamp which provided a central current of air through the burner, thus allowing the more perfect combustion of the gas issuing from the wick. It was a significant improvement on the traditional oil lamp.

The new Cromer light was shone for the first time on 8 September 1792. At the time it was one of only two lights identified by an intermittent self-identifying flash.

Trinity House took over management of the lighthouse on 29 September 1822, with two young women acting as keepers.

The clay cliffs would not hold fast, and after several landslips, the Foulness lighthouse went the way of Clayton's tower on 7 December 1866, after being left standing precariously on the edge of a precipice for several days before. Most of Foulness Point went with it.

The destruction of the lighthouse had been predicted more than three decades before, and in 1832 a decision was made to build a replacement and let nature take its course with the old one.

The existing Cromer lighthouse, its octagonal 59ft tower standing 275ft above sea level, was built from stone half a mile back from the cliff edge. Twice as powerful as its predecessor, it came into operation on 29 June 1833.

It was supplied with gas from 1905, replacing the oil burners and increasing its 36,000 candlepower to 49,000 candlepower, with modified equipment, producing a flash every 30 seconds.

Electricity arrived in 1935, and from then until 1958, a combination of gas burners and electric lamps provided illumination.

In 1958, Cromer was the last lighthouse in England to still be using the catoptric system of lighting, with placing reflectors behind the light source. The lantern was removed and replaced with a smaller one with a prismatic lens, and converted to all-electric operation. After five months in the dark, it returned to action on 6 November 1958.

In June 1990 the lighthouse was converted to automatic operation. The white light flashes every five seconds, and is visible for 24 miles.

The two-storey keepers' cottages alongside the tower are let out as holiday apartments although the property is still owned by Trinity House.

A 1905 postcard of Cromer lighthouse.
ROBIN JONES COLLECTION

The stripy bands of the High Light date from 1883. ROBIN JONES

CHAPTER ELEVEN
HAPPISBURGH LIGHTS

Windy Old Weather
As we were a-fishing off Haisborough light,
Shooting and hauling and trawling all night,

(Chorus)
It was windy old weather, stormy old weather,
When the wind blows, we all pull together.

We sighted a herring, the king of the sea,
Says "Now, old skipper, you cannot catch me."

We sighted a mackerel with stripes on his back,
"Time, now, old skipper, to shift your main tack."

We sighted a conger as long as a mile.
"Wind's blowing easterly," he said with a smile.

We sighted a plaice that had spots on his side,
Says "Now, old skipper, these seas you won't ride."

I think what the fishes are saying is right.
We'll haul in our nets and we'll make for the Light.

HAPPISBURGH HIGH LIGHT fits the archetypal image of a lighthouse, tall and striped with red and white bands like a piece of candy floss, and eminently suitable for any cartoon-comic depiction of the British seaside.

It is easily one of Norfolk's most prominent coastal landmarks, although the village from which it takes its name, pronounced 'Hazeborough', stands above the cliffs in the far-flung north-eastern extremity of the county.

Opposite: *Happisburgh High Light is one of the iconic landmark buildings of Norfolk.* ROBIN JONES

Its origins lie in the great storm of October 1789, when 600 sailors drowned and around 70 ships were lost off the Norfolk coast.

At the time there were the fire beacons at Cromer and Caister and a candle-powered light at Winterton to guide mariners, but nothing off Happisburgh, where lie the treacherous Haisbro Sands and where a real need was quickly albeit lately identified.

Trinity House responded almost immediately by building a pair of lighthouses 400 yards apart. On a hill back from the coast, the 85ft tall High Light was built, while on the lower cliff tops, the 20ft shorter Low Light was erected.

The first lights were shone in both on the evening of 1 January 1791. They were fixed lights, each powered by an array of Argand oil lamps positioned in front of polished reflectors.

Ships had to line up both lights in order to enter the sheltered waters between the sands and the shore from the south.

The coat of arms of Trinity House.
ROBIN JONES

A few months before, a lightship was established at Newarp on the southern edge of Haisboro Sands 17 miles to the south.

In 1832, the northern end of the sands was marked by the Haisboro lightship, which was moored 12 miles off the coast. It showed a pair of white fixed lights 36ft above sea level, with a range of ten miles.

A new radical design of lantern was installed in 1863. Consisting of diagonal frames which cross each other at a constant angle so that mariners can view the light from all angles to seaward, it is still there today.

Improvements were made to both lighthouses in 1868, with the Birmingham firm of Chance Brothers supplying prismatic glass optics to replace the older system. One oil lamp could be placed in front of each optic, as opposed to needing a lamp for each reflector as had been the case. The new optics gave the High Light an increased range of 17 miles and the Low Light 15 miles.

In 1872, coal gas lighting was introduced on an experimental basis by inventor John Wigram. The gas was manufactured in the grounds of the High Light, with coal being brought in by sea.

The gas lights at the High Light appeared brighter than the oil lamps at the Low Light, but Trinity House, fought shy of converting more lighthouses to coal gas. Nevertheless, the gas system at Happisburgh remained in use for more than three decades, until a paraffin vapour burner was installed in 1904.

A third lightship, the Would, was established in 1880.

Right: *A rare surviving depiction of the Low Light, taken from an Admiralty chart of the 1880s. This drawing also appears in* The Book of Happisburgh *by Mary Trett and Richard Hoggett, and also published by Halsgrove.*

Far right: *The remains of the Low Light on the beach at Happisburgh.*
RONALD JAMES

By the 1880s, it became clear that the sea had eaten into the cliffs to such an extent that the survival of the Low Light was threatened. In 1883, Trinity House decided to declare it redundant, and install a clockwork-operating occulting light in the high tower, which was painted in the striped bands for the first time.

The Low Light was sold by tender in 1886 and after its equipment was salvaged, it was demolished. Its Chance Brothers optic was recycled for use in Southwold's lighthouse.

In 1929, Happisburgh became the fifth manned lighthouse to be converted to an acetylene-powered light in a bid to cut labour costs. The resident keepers were declared redundant, although it was still necessary to check the light from time to time. The keepers' cottages were sold off as private homes.

Mains electricity was installed in 1947. A 500-watt lamp with a range of 18 miles was introduced, with a diesel generator as back-up, although the acetylene system was held in reserve for emergencies. The light was altered to a sequence of three white flashes every 30 seconds.

In the late fifties, coastal erosion exposed the foundations of the Low Light which tumbled

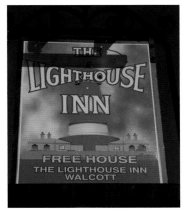

Happisburgh High Light is celebrated in the name of the Lighthouse Inn at nearby Walcott. ROBIN JONES

One of the later Haisboro Sands lightships. ROBIN JONES COLLECTION

on to the beach, and can still be seen at very low tides today.

In 1988 Trinity House announced that it was to close both the High Light and the Haisboro Sands lightship, which would be superseded by a navigational buoy, on 13 June.

Locals were aghast, and protests persuaded Trinity House to order a rethink about the future of the lighthouse.

A local trust was formed to save it and keep it operational, fishermen arguing that merely extending the range of Cromer lighthouse would not be sufficient.

Trinity House had the power to pass on a working lighthouse, but only to another lighthouse authority.

So inviting, but sandbanks off Happisburgh's beach have proven deadly. MIKE LAWRENCE*

Undeterred, the trust set itself up as a statutory lighthouse authority, after a Private Members Bill took 17 months to go through Parliament, the necessary legislation was passed. The Happisburgh Lighthouse Bill received Royal Assent on 25 April 1990, and it took control of the light from 1 August that year.

A few days before, Her Majesty Queen Elizabeth the Queen Mother visited both the lighthouse and the parish church. Her brother Michael Bowes Lyon had owned the village at one stage.

Later that month, the BBC's *Challenge Anneka* with Anneka Rice organised the painting of the lighthouse inside and out in just 36 hours. The drive was also relaid and the back-up battery replaced. The following year, the trust introduced open days.

Although Trinity House retained ownership of the High Light, it is maintained and operated by the Happisburgh Lighthouse Trust. Princess Anne became its patron and visited the lighthouse on 12 May 2010 to mark two decades of its independent operation.

It is still very much a working lighthouse today, although it has far greater relevance to local fishermen and yachtsmen than larger vessels who rely on GPS and other high-tech aids.

The tower is open for guided tours on selected Sunday afternoons in the summer, or visits by prior arrangement.

CHAPTER TWELVE
WINTERTON-ON-SEA AND CAISTER

WINTERTON NESS WAS in the heyday of sail the most feared obstacle on the east coast between Newcastle and London.

The huge sandbank, far greater in extent than today, stretched out into Yarmouth Roads, the seaway into the port of Great Yarmouth.

It has proved so deadly over the centuries that the settlement of Winterton largely comprises homes built out of wood from the many shipwrecks that had taken place here.

We have the great eighteenth-century writer Daniel Defoe to thank for a graphic description of the village as he saw it during his visit of 1722.

Already he had famously referred to Winterton's lighthouse in his earlier novel *Robinson Crusoe*. However, when he came to see the site for himself, he found that Winterton had four.

Responding to grave concerns about Winterton Ness, Trinity House surveyed Yarmouth Roads in 1600 to see what could be done.

Two candle-powered lighthouses were built to the south at Caister, but little is known about them, apart from their claim to being the first to be authorised on the English coast, and they have long since disappeared. There have been suggestions that the Romans had a lighthouse at their settlement at Caister, but there is no evidence of one.

This first lighthouse at Winterton was built as a result of a petition presented by Sir William Erskine and a Dr Welwood.

James I, who had been schooled with Erskine's sons, readily granted the petition, to the anger of Trinity House, which had seen no need for a lighthouse at Winterton itself. Trinity House mounted a legal challenge which caused the Erskine scheme to be delayed. In the meantime, Trinity House despatched its own delegation to use its statutory powers to build its own lighthouse at Winterton. Work on the Tower lighthouse began in March 1616 and took three months to complete, tolls on passing ships being made free for the first ten months.

At the same time, soldier John Meldrum, who was later knighted by James for his military service, bought out Dr Welwood's share in the Erksine scheme.

The earlier dispute was resolved by a new Attorney General, Sir Henry Yelverton, who upheld Trinity House's exclusive rights to build lighthouses, with the caveat that the monarch could give permission to other bodies to do so if he saw fit.

The new lantern added to the top of Winterton lighthouse in 2011. ROBIN JONES

Erskine and Meldrum were granted a patent for a Winterton lighthouse of their own on 18 February 1617.

Livid, Trinity House, advised seafarers not to pay tolls to Erskine and Meldrum, and offered lower dues.

Once the patent had been obtained, Erskine and Medrum's contingent forced their way into the Tower lighthouse and lit their own lights in it while awaiting the completion of their own lighthouses.

The Privy Council ordered an inquiry, and Erskine and Meldrum argued that their action in seeking the rights to build a lighthouse at Winterton had been made necessary because of the earlier refusal of Trinity House to provide one.

Meldrum's arguments at the hearing won the day, and for the next 16 years, his right to the lights was confirmed. Trinity House was barred from erecting any light within two miles of Winterton.

The lights consisted of a beacon near the village and two leading lights set up in towers built on the sandbank itself.

Meldrum went on to win permission to build a lighthouse at Orford Ness in Suffolk in 1634, and subsequently sold the rights of both to London alderman Gerard Gore, who in

The new-look Winterton lighthouse behind holiday accommodation on the adjacent Hermanus holidays complex, which has been designed in the style of traditional Norfolk thatched round houses. ROBIN JONES

Winterton lighthouse in operational days.

1637, obtained a new lease on both covering half a century.

A series of storms in the 1670s changed the shape of the coast, leaving a new deeper channel leading into Yarmouth Roads. In 1677, Trinity House obtained permission to build an extra small candle-powered lighthouse on the shore to act as a front light in conjunction with the Tower lighthouse.

The silly situation whereby both lighthouse owners charged separate tolls arose.

Even worse, within six years, coastal erosion was threatening the survival of the new lighthouse, which Trinity House had physically hauled further up the beach.

In 1686, the small or low lighthouse was again threatened, but to move it again, and use it as a lower light to the privately-owned Tower lighthouse, both would have to be moved. Eventually its owner Sir Edward Turnour agreed, and so in 1687, a new octagonal tower 70ft high was built on the edge of a low cliff 20ft above the high tide mark.

The lower light was moved, and both were relit on 12 September 1687.

The pair and the two on the Ness, known as the Thwart Lights and which were by that time principally maintained for the benefit of local fishermen, comprised the four lights recorded by Defoe.

Turnour received "1d. per ton for every vessel sailing by" as his dues.

The storm of the night of 31 October 1789 caused numerous shipwrecks and loss of life, and the subsequent inquiry found that mariners had confused the pairs of lights at Winterton and Caister, and set in motion moves which led to the building of Happisburgh lighthouse.

Winterton lighthouse with its World War Two lookout. STAVROS

In turn, Happisburgh spelled the end for the Winterton low light. Trinity House also demanded that the owner of the Tower lighthouse, Lord Braybrooke, who also owned Orford Ness, made major improvements, beginning with its conversion from coal to oil burning.

These were carried out and the new light was shone on November 23 1791 for the first time. It shone a continuous light which could be seen 14 miles out to sea.

The Thwart Lights were allowed to fall into disuse around the 1820s, and were pulled down around 1830.

An Act of Parliament in 1836 ended private ownership of lighthouses. Four years later, its new owner Trinity House built a new red-painted 62ft brick and stone circular tower to replace Turnour's lighthouse which was then knocked down. The new light was shone for the first time in early autumn 1840, and standing 97ft above the waves, could be seen from 17 miles.

In 1843, earlier proposals for a lightship at Cockle Gatt or Cockle Sand between Winterton and Caister were implemented.

Winterton lighthouse received a new prismatic lens and Argand burner in the 1860s, replacing the oil lamps and reflectors. A first order optic was supplied by Chance Brothers.

In the late nineteenth century, marram grass was planted along the sandy shore of Winterton in a bid to prevent erosion. In a reversal of what happened elsewhere at places like Cromer, the effect saw land reclaimed rather than conceded to the sea and the lighthouse appeared to move inland, eventually to the tune of 400 yards!

Between a new barrier of marram-planted dunes and the cliff on which the lighthouse was built, a trough took shape, and is now known as the Valley.

Left so far from the waves, Winterton lighthouse became increasingly less useful.

During World War One, the lighthouse became a military lookout post.

The prevalence of lightships and buoys now guarding Yarmouth Roads led to it finally being declared redundant in 1921, its light shining for the final time in August that year.

The lighthouse was auctioned off in early 1922, having lost its lantern. One report suggested the equipment was reused in a lighthouse in the Bahamas. The tower and its keeper's cottage, repainted white, became a private holiday home, a circular observation room being built where the lantern had been.

Again used as a military lookout by the Winterton Emergency Coastal Battery during World War Two, the tower was strengthened with brick and concrete above the level of the observation room, and a gallery was added.

On 9 January 1940, the Trinity House unarmed service vessel *Reculver* was badly damaged by enemy action after supplying the Cockle lightship, some crew members of which were on board. A Dornier attacked the *Reculver* with bombs and machine guns. A bomb exploded on the boat deck where the off-duty lightship crew were standing, killing second officer George Purvis and wounding 55 men.

Disabled, the *Reculver* was towed into Great Yarmouth where Trinity House had a depot on South Quay, her funnel riddled with bullet holes, in an attack that predated that on the East Dudgeon lightship by three weeks.

She was repaired, but on 14 October that year struck a mine in the mouth of the Humber and sank. Her master, Captain J. J. Woolnough, was made an MBE.

When peace returned, Winterton lighthouse became the home of East Norfolk MP Viscount Elmley. It was later sold to the adjacent holiday park, and in 2000 the lighthouse and cottage were on the market again, becoming two private dwellings. The tower was up for sale again in 2005.

The current owner of the lighthouse had made extensive renovations, the most dramatic being, in 2011, the removal of the brick lookout and its replacement with a new lantern, to a new design bearing little resemblance to the 1840 or 1868 lanterns, although it still remains inoperative.

Winterton, incidentally, became on-Sea from 1953, to distinguish it from Winterton in Lincolnshire.

CHAPTER THIRTEEN
GORLESTON AND HOPTON

GREAT YARMOUTH grew up on a thin spit created by the River Yare taking a sudden turn southwards rather than flowing straight out to sea. The river estuary forms the town's harbour, with Gorleston-on-Sea on the opposite bank.

By the eighteenth century, it was a thriving herring port, and was also visited by Daniel Defoe. He described the harbour as follows: "It is plac'd on a peninsula between the River Yare and the sea; the two last lying parallel to one another, and the town in the middle: The river lies on the west-side of the town, and being grown very large and deep, by a conflux of all the rivers on this side the county, forms the haven; and the town facing to the west also, and open to the river, makes the finest key (quay) in England, if not in Europe, not inferior even to that of Marseilles itself."

Its suburb Gorleston was a port town at the time of the Domesday Book and also became a major fishing port, with salt pans for producing salt to preserve the fish.

Historically part of Suffolk, it was moved into Norfolk when it merged with Great Yarmouth in 1835.

The two settlements sit on opposite sides of the great harbour, known as the Haven, with two lighthouses to guide the way in.

In 1676, Charles II gave permission for a lighthouse to be built at Gorleston, but it seems unlikely one was built at that time. Later, a light was displayed on the South Denes, the southern part of the spit on which Great Yarmouth stands, to guide ships into the mouth of the harbour. It was a basic form of lighthouse akin to a brazier on top of an elevated framework surmounted by an open fire.

A fixed limit light was established on Gorleston South Pier in 1852.

The 20ft tall hexagonal white iron and close-boarded wooden tower lighthouse with canopied top and gallery and a traditional light that appeared on so many Edwardian postcards when the pier was a favourite sunspot for holidaymakers, was demolished in 1955, along with the pier. This lighthouse displayed a red light while the tide was coming in, and a green light when it went out until the water had fallen to one foot on the tide gauge. The lights were not shone when choppy water made the harbour entrance dangerous.

A new pier was built and its lighthouse was replaced by a two-storey square brick and concrete structure built as a harbourmaster's office and later relocated to this spot. Also located at the end of the pier, this structure has a roof-mounted light which emits a red flash every three seconds. On the roof are also communications equipment, the harbour control lights, and the foghorn which sounds three blasts every 60 seconds.

The building is now a Coastwatch station, and home to the Gorleston branch of the National Coastwatch Institution. This voluntary organisation and registered charity, which is totally separate from the Coastguard service, keeps visual watch along Britain's coasts. It was set up in Cornwall in 1994 following the deaths of two local fishermen who drowned beneath a recently-closed Coastguard station at Bass Point. Most Coastguard visual watch stations were closed following a period of rationalisation.

The Gorleston station has more than 60 volunteer members who watch the sea from 8am to 7pm in the winter and to 9.30pm in the summer, seven days a week.

Inside the harbour stands the 69ft unpainted brick tower of the Gorleston (Range Rear) lighthouse which dates from 14 April 1887 when the first stone was ceremonially laid by the mayor of Yarmouth.

It was designed by local architect Dudley Arnott and built by Thomas George Leggett on land acquired by the Port & Haven Commissioners at Pier Marsh near Brush Bend, the point where the Yare estuary makes a right-angle bend just before entering the sea.

Trinity House consulting engineer Sir James Douglass inspected the site and recommended that the light should burn gas rather than oil.

The lighthouse was refurbished in 1957. With a focal plane of 66ft, it displays a continuous red light through the river mouth with a range of six miles.

The rear light of the harbour entrance range is mounted low on the tower. This light

The Range Rear lighthouse stands in a parade of small shops. ROBIN JONES

Opposite: *Gorleston's brick Range Rear lighthouse tower at Brush Bend.* ROBIN JONES

The mid-Fifties South Pier lighthouse.
ROBIN JONES

A Raphael Tuck early twentieth-century postcard view of the old South Pier lighthouse. ROBIN JONES
COLLECTION

displays a white light four seconds on and two seconds off.

The height of the lights was fixed by local fisherman Harvey George. He went out to sea and using a pole sighted on the Brush Quay with two black balls hoisted on it, gauged the correct height for the lights, 25ft and 64ft above high water mark.

Both lighthouses are operated by the Great Yarmouth Port Authority.

To the south of Gorleston lies Hopton-on-Sea, where a pair of lighthouses was built in 1865 to lead ships away from Corton Sands.

Hopton's high light was erected to the east of the former railway station while the low light was built on Hopton Denes, a row of dunes long since carried away by the waves.

Again, shifting sands and changing currents saw the sands extend southwards and by 1871 the Hopton lights could no longer be aligned and were declared redundant and demolished.

In 2003, the Trinity House depot on Yarmouth's South Quay which had serviced lighthouses, lightships and buoys, was closed after 160 years. For lightship spotters, the waters off Great Yarmouth would have been a happy hunting ground prior to automation, with vessels based at Cockle, Cross Sand, Corton and furthest out of all, Smiths Knoll, 27 miles from the shore, with Newarp, Would and Haisbro to the north.

A ship enters the Haven, with the South Pier light to the right. ROBIN JONES

CHAPTER FOURTEEN
LOWESTOFT

LOWESTOFT NOT ONLY contains the easternmost point of Britain, but is the proud home of England's oldest official light station, which dates from 1609.

Lights and navigational aids have been vital to Lowestoft's prosperity as a major fishing port, with herrings its trademark until the twentieth century.

As with other ports on the coast of East Anglia, the town has suffered from coastal erosion. Easton Ness was once the easternmost point, but over the centuries was denuded to the extent

Lowestoft lighthouse stands on top of a ridge with unrivalled views of the sea lanes it serves. TRINITY HOUSE

Lowestoft lighthouse and keepers' cottages as viewed from Yarmouth Road today. ROBIN JONES

that Lowestoft Ness took the honour. However, Lowestoft also gained from this process.

Debris from cliffs washed away from the tide has to go somewhere, and at Lowestoft, the sea built up what is known as the Beach. It was here that Lowestoft's fishing community had its roots.

As at Great Yarmouth, a row of sandbanks lies out to sea, with Lowestoft Roads forming a navigable channel. Access to it from the shore was through a gap in the Holme Bank and Barnard Sand known as the Stanford Channel.

A man named Bushell is believed to have built early lighthouses at Caister and Lowestoft, but Trinity House took legal action which meant that he had to take out leases on them.

In 1609, Trinity House took over responsibility for the Lowestoft lights. It proposed to erect two towers, a high and low light "for the direction of ships which crept by night in the dangerous passage betwixt Lowestoft and Winterton". A pair of timber structures with candle-powered lanterns duly were built at Lowestoft Ness. When lined up, they indicated the deepest water of Stanford Channel.

The pair needed to be rebuilt in 1628 and again in 1676. That was the year in which the great diarist Samuel Pepys became Master of Trinity House, and one of his first acts was to

LOWESTOFT, SUFFOLK

EAST COAST LANDMARKS

BRITISH RAILWAYS   SEE BRITAIN BY TRAIN

British Railways poster depicting Lowestoft lighthouse.
ROBIN JONES COLLECTION

A panoramic view of 1764 showing Lowestoft's sea front with the low light.

Lowestoft's low lighthouse was discontinued in 1923. MIKE MILLICHAMP COLLLECTION

order an inspection of the Lowestoft lights.

A new brick-built high lighthouse which burned coal was erected on top of the ridge behind the Beach, so it could no longer be confused with lights from nearby houses, and the lower light was moved so it was in alignment with it.

The new high light could now be seen from much further away, and became a major navigational aid to long-distance seafarers, rather than just of value to local fishermen. It was as useful as Sir John Clayton's light at Corton to the south. That fact had not been lost on him, and he had already objected to Trinity House building the new replacement light on the hill.

After a legal wrangle lasting three years, Trinity House dealt a death blow to Clayton's business at Corton, by making the Lowestoft lights toll free. Within 12 months, his tower was abandoned, and he passed on his interests at Corton to a Henry Bowyer, who obtained permission to establish two leading lights at the entrance to St Nicholas Gat, using the old tower. It seems that the venture quickly died a death.

Pepys arranged for a plaque carrying not only the Trinity House coat of arms but that of his family to be fixed to the new high lighthouse. It reads: "Erected by the brotherhood of Trinity House, Deptford Strond in the Mastership of Samuel Pepys, Esq., Secretary of Ye Admiralty of England A.D. 1676." It is preserved inside the modern-day version.

Following representations from townsfolk, the high light was enclosed by a lantern the following year, to eliminate the risk of sparks setting fire to the surrounding wooden houses.

Even so, other buildings continued to be erected around the lighthouse, and in 1688 Trinity House ordered the tower to be raised by 10ft.

Close-up view of the South Pier lighthouse. ROBIN JONES

Stormy seas break over the harbour entrance. ROBIN JONES COLLECTION

The pier lighthouses guarding the narrow harbour entrance.
ROBIN JONES

Opposite: Lowestoft Harbour and its pier lighthouses in the last great age of sail. ROBIN JONES COLLECTION

Trinity House discontinued the low light in 1706 because of encroachment by the sea, leading to many years of complaints that this action had made the navigation of the Stanford Channel more difficult. It was not until 1730 that a new low light was provided.

Made of timber and holding a lantern containing three oil burners, it was designed to be portable. It could be moved every time the channel changed its course, to be in alignment with the higher light.

The high light's coal fire was replaced in 1777 by a circle of oil lamps and an experimental complex reflector system, later described as the 'Spangle light', which had 4000 small square mirrors and a vastly improved range of 20 miles. The principle was much the same as a glittering mirror ball set into the roof of a nightclub or discotheque, which reflects spotlights and laser lights as it turns.

It lasted in service for around 19 years. While it seemed impressive at first, the light intensity was lost because there was no way of concentrating the rays into a single beam.

The silvered parabolic reflector system developed by King's Lynn-based physicist Ezekial Walker and so gainfully employed at Hunstanton, in combination with the new oil burners invented by Swiss engineer Amie Argand, brought a sudden end to spangle lights.

The Lowestoft keepers objected to losing a light which was still based around a fire –

A 1923 view of the St Nicholas lightship, which was moored off Corton near Lowestoft. It was also known as Hewett Channel and St Nicholas Gat, and was Admiralty List of Lights No. 141. The station was subsequently discontinued. ANN MATTHEWS

Standing near Lowestoft Lighthouse and built to the same height is the town's Royal Naval Patrol Service memorial in Belle Vue Park. It was designed so that the lighthouse beam illuminates the gilded sailing ship on the top. TIM PARKINSON*

because they were left with no means of drying their clothes after trudging through the rain to attend the low light, which was rebuilt again in 1779.

By this time, the coastline was changing again, with the Stanford Channel becoming shallower, and great sandbanks forming offshore. At the turn of the century, the pattern changed again, with the sandbar vanishing and Lowestoft Ness taking a pounding again. The low light was rebuilt in 1803 with a bigger lantern and, in 1827, it was found to be at risk of being undermined by the sea. A replacement with a brick foundation displayed its light for the first time on 25 February 1832.

Meanwhile, technology was moving forward faster than Trinity House realised. The widespread use of oil for lighting homes meant that the lights from neighbouring houses in Lowestoft were brighter than the high light. The response? Householders were asked to keep their windows shuttered at night so mariners would not mistake them for the lighthouse.

In 1840, it was discovered that high light keeper John Bishop attended each night only to light the lamps, then went moonlighting to work in a nearby pub. Both Bishop and his assistant were sacked on the spot.

Following experiments with electric lighting at South Foreland lighthouse and Dungeness in Kent, in 1870 the decision was taken to electrify the Lowestoft high light.

The existing tower was not considered strong enough to hold the necessary equipment and so a new 52ft white-painted round brick tower was built. This is the lighthouse we see today.

It was not electrified at that time as planned, because paraffin oil suddenly became available as an illuminant, and was shown to be economical and efficient.

However, a new optical system with a revolving lens was fitted and from then on the light flashed at half-minute intervals from when the work was completed in 1874.

The low light was moved 80 yards back due to erosion of the shore in 1881, and its attendant keepers' cottages were washed away. A decision was taken to make it an unmanned station, while it and the high light were connected to the town's coal gas mains supply for the first time.

The low light was moved again in 1894, and afterwards a series of sea defences finally held back the forces of nature, but only as far as the protected shore was concerned. The knock-on effect was greater pressure to bear on the cliffs to the south of the sea wall, where around 100 homes at Pakefield disappeared into the sea, and the Stanford Channel vanished altogether.

That made the low light obsolete, and it was finally discontinued in August 1923.

Lowestoft high light overlooks the easternmost point of the British Isles, depicted here. There really is nothing more to it! ROBIN JONES

The high light was electrified in July 1936, and given powerful twin optical lenses. During both world wars, the light was turned off, apart from occasions when it was needed to guide naval vessels. Apart from this, Lowestoft can be proud that it has shone lights for mariners officially for more than four centuries without a break, and probably for several years before.

In 1976 the light was automated and the timing functions were taken over by electronics.

The focal plane of the lighthouse is 121ft, that is, the distance from sea level to the focus of the light. It flashes white every 15 seconds and can be seen from 17 miles.

From above, the lighthouse marks Lowestoft Ness. However, those who are familiar with the theme park that is Land's End, the westernmost point of the British mainland, the serpentine souvenir shops of Lizard Point, the southernmost tip, or the landmark of John O' Groats Hotel in the north, will be sorely disappointed here. Visitors who manage to wind their way through an industrial estate will find a flat piece of tarmac with a dial setting out compass points to other parts of Europe, and that's your lot.

The lighthouse towers above Sparrow's Nest Park and the Lowestoft Maritime Museum, which occasionally offers visits to the light station. The museum contains the pre-1976 mechanism from the lighthouse.

Dating from 1847, there is a twin pair of white-painted lighthouses guarding the narrow entrance to Lowestoft Harbour.

Both 30ft hexagonal cylindrical brick towers with a lantern and a gallery, rising from the centre of a single-storey pavilion, they have focal planes of 39ft. The North Pier lighthouse shows a green light, four seconds on, one second off, while the South Pier light shows a red light with a similar pattern. The South Pier lighthouse has a foghorn which emits four blasts every minute.

Both are operated by the Port of Lowestoft and are visible for six miles.

A light buoy displayed near to Lowestoft Maritime Museum. ROBIN JONES

CHAPTER FIFTEEN
PAKEFIELD AND KESSINGLAND

THE COASTLINE OF East Anglia is, as we have seen, not only subject to severe coastal erosion, but rapid changes. One winter storm can alter the course of a shipping channel, rendering previous navigational aids useless overnight.

In July 1831, Trinity House in London despatched a part of elder brethren to look into the possibility of establishing subsidary lights around Lowestoft.

Reporting back, the group recommended that such a light should be built at Pakefield two miles to the south, to assist ships through the narrow channel between Barnard and Newcome sandbanks.

London architect Richard Suter was commissioned to design the lighthouse which was erected by Great Yarmouth builder James Taylor on top of a 34ft sandy cliff in the grounds of Pakefield Hall, along with two keepers' cottages.

Its 30ft brick circular tower had a lantern containing two Argand lamps. Their fixed red light was first shone on 1 May 1832 and could be seen for nine miles.

For the next 18 years, a legal wrangle raged between the landowner and Trinity House, with the cost of providing the access road being a particular sticking point.

Short in height, and short in life. The shifting channels moved again, and by 1850 Pakefield's stumpy lighthouse was ineffective.

A new lighthouse was built three miles to the south on the cliffs at Kessingland.

Pakefield's light was turned off on 1 December 1864, and Kessingland's tower existed only into the early years of the twentieth century. No trace of it now remains.

Pakefield lighthouse fell derelict and in 1929 was sold back to Howard Barrett, the owner of Pakefield Hall for £150.

In the twenties, Barrett opened the Pakefield Hall holiday camp. At first it was made up of tents standing in farmland, but in the thirties, wooden chalets were introduced.

Part of the lighthouse and its keepers' cottages were given a new lease of life as a campers' bar.

A wall-mounted lifebelt showing that Pakefield lighthouse is once again playing a role in maritime safety more than 150 years after its light was switched off. ROBIN JONES

With the winds of war gathering pace, in April 1938 the Royal Observer Corps moved into the lighthouse.

The roof and lantern were removed to allow a clearer view of both overhead aircraft approaching and sea movements.

In World War Two, the holiday camp was used as a transit camp for troops and refugees, while Auxiliary Territorial Service women were billeted in the keepers' cottages.

On 12 May 1943, the lighthouse was machine-gunned by the Luftwaffe during a raid on Lowestoft and in October 1944 a faulty V1 flying bomb fell into the sea at the foot of the cliff on which the lighthouse stands.

The lighthouse's military role ceased in 1945. After Pontin's bought the holiday camp in 1958, the lighthouse later became a darkroom for the camp photographer.

Pontin's still owns the camp and the lighthouse. In 2000, local volunteers renovated the lighthouse as a Coastwatch station, with local people giving up their spare time to perform surveillance duties which until recent times were carried out by Coastguards, and appeals for more helpers are frequently made.

The access road that was at the heart of the legal dispute in the mid nineteenth century is now the A12 trunk road.

Pakefield lighthouse today, used as a Coastwatch station. ROBIN JONES

CHAPTER SIXTEEN
SOUTHWOLD

SOUTHWOLD LIGHTHOUSE with its round white tower is easily one of the most distinctive on the coastline of East Anglia, and also unusual in that it is not only built well back from the sea, but stands in the middle of a town, surrounded by houses. It was also built fairly late in the day.

Following the effective destruction of Orford's Low lighthouse in a fierce storm of 1887, as we will see in Chapter 17, Trinity House decided not to build a replacement but look for an altogether new site for a light.

Southwold was chosen because it stood out on high ground in a locality largely comprising a low shoreline and flat marshes.

The beautiful 'village green' setting of Southwold lighthouse. ROBIN JONES

Aerial view of Southwold lighthouse.
TRINITY HOUSE

The 101ft tower of Southwold lighthouse. ROBIN JONES

It was decided to build a 101ft brick tower on land next to the Coastguard station, but while waiting for it to be finished, from 19 February 1889, a temporary light was shone from a wooden structure on California Sands. The town celebrated its inauguration with a band playing the National Anthem, with good reason, for 283 shipwrecks were recorded along this stretch of coast in the nineteenth century. Local fishermen formed beach companies to salvage valuables from wrecked ships and to pick up survivors, while in 1840, volunteers founded the Southwold Lifeboat Society.

Sir James Douglass, engineer in chief to Trinity House, best known for the design and construction of the fourth Eddystone Lighthouse, for which he was knighted, supervised the building of the permanent Southwold lighthouse which began in May 1889.

The chosen site was praised because the smoke from the town's chimney's would not obscure the light, which has a focal plane of 122ft, the lantern and gallery being well above the rooftops of local houses.

Town mayor Eustace Grubb, laid the first of 1,500,000 half bricks which were delivered via Halesworth on the Southwold Railway, a line built to the unusual 3ft gauge and which became a legend in its own lifetime due to music hall jokes about its reliability.

The transport of building materials was all but too much for the little railway, which joined the main Great Eastern Railway at Halesworth eight miles to the west. The railway and

The lantern of Southwold lighthouse.
MARTIN PETTITT*

The 113-step spiral staircase.
ELJAY*

Southwold in the 1940s, when there were far fewer cars to clutter the view of the lighthouse. ROBIN JONES COLLECTION

the local coal merchant, Thomas Moy & Company, had just 15 freight wagons between them, and had to mount an almost non-stop shuttle service.

The eight-ton lantern arrived from Harwich ten months later in two sections, carried in two of Thomas Moy's wagons.

The lighthouse, which is attached to a two-storey keeper's cottage, came on stream on 3 September 1890. Six days later, the six-wick Argand oil burner burst into flames and was destroyed, the new keepers' inexperience being blamed. They were retrained and the burner was replaced, but in 1906 it was superseded by a Matthews incandescent oil burner.

A Hood 100mm petroleum vapour burner was installed in 1923 and provided illumination until the lighthouse was electrified in 1938, when the keepers were withdrawn.

The lighthouse provides a waymark for ships navigating the east coast and guides vessels heading for Southwold Harbour.

Two red sectors mark shoals to the north and the Sizewell Bank to the south, and are visible over land north and south for 15 nautical miles, while the main navigation light is white and visible for 18 nautical miles. Since 1965, a 1,500-watt lamp emits four flashes every 20 seconds.

Opposite: The lighthouse towers above the Sole Bay Inn. ROBIN JONES

An attendant visits the lighthouse regularly to conduct routine maintenance.

In 2005, a Trinity House report suggested that 11 of 69 remaining lighthouses in England and Wales could be closed if GPS technology and radio navigation back-up were good enough, and most sailors by then routinely used such navigation aids. Southwold and Lowestoft were on the list of 11.

However, in 2009, the threat of closure was lifted, after Trinity House conceded that GPS was "not considered robust or available enough" at that time.

A listed building, the lighthouse stands at the St James Green end of Stradbroke Road.

Interior tours lasting around 20 minutes are organised by Southwold Millennium Foundation under licence from Trinity House. Visitors can climb the 113 steps for some of the best panoramic views in Suffolk.

Southwold lighthouse has become a defining icon of the town, one of the more genteel seaside resorts. Scores of artists visit the town to paint it, and nearby Adnams Brewery has named beers after it.

The 350-year-old Swan Hotel in recent years refurbished 16 rooms around its garden and renamed them the Lighthouse Rooms, as you can see the tower from the site.

It truly is a king of lighthouses!

To the south of Southwold lies Aldeburgh. Tower Mill, a nineteenth-century windmill on the shore long since converted into a house, often wrongly described as a lighthouse. The town does have one, however: in two-dimensional form — on the gable wall of the Lighthouse Restaurant! BRIAN WESTLAKE*

CHAPTER SEVENTEEN
ORFORD NESS

THE DALEKS, MAYBE the Klingons, or perhaps just ordinary everyday little green men from Mars, landed in Suffolk in late December 1980.

They were seen by dozens of US Air Force staff at nearby RAF Bentwaters and RAF Woodbridge over a two or three-day period. And in the true spirit of every good science fiction story, the whole affair was hushed up by the authorities to prevent mass panic.

Indeed, the powers that be passed off the multiple sightings of strange lights coming through the trees in Rendlesham Forest as stars in the night sky, a fireball, or maybe plain old Orford Ness lighthouse just doing its job, as local forester Vince Thurkettle suggested.

The Rendlesham Forest Incident is regarded by ufologists and conspiracy theorists as the most famous UFO event to have happened in Britain.

The Ministry of Defence did itself little favours by at first denying that it had investigated the strange lights as a security matter, only for it to later emerge that it had built up a substantial file.

The incident which took place between 24-27 December began when guards at RAF Woodbridge noticed mysterious lights appearing to descend into the forest, and then moved amongst the trees. The lighthouse is along the same line of sight but five miles further to the east of the forest.

The story was first broken by the *News of the World* in 1983.

One of the USAF personnel, Sergeant Jim Penniston, later claimed to have encountered a "craft of unknown origin" and to have made detailed notes of its features, touched its "warm" surface, and copied the numerous symbols on its body. The object allegedly flew away after their 45-minute encounter.

He also claimed to have seen triangular landing gear on the object, leaving three impressions in the ground that were visible the next day. In 1994, he underwent regression hypnosis and claimed that the "craft" he encountered had come from our future, and had been flown by time travellers, not aliens.

The deputy base commander, Lieutenant Colonel Charles I. Halt, 30 years later signed a public document in which he himself stated that he believed the object to be extraterrestrial, and that both the UK and US government had covered up the incident "by the use of well-

Orford Ness lighthouse today, standing sentinel above the shifting shingle – but for how long? TRINITY HOUSE

practiced methods of disinformation."

More importantly for us here, he waved aside claims that he had confused a UFO with a lighthouse beam. "While in Rendlesham Forest, our security team observed a light that looked like a large eye, red in color, moving through the trees. After a few minutes this object began dripping something that looked like molten metal.

"A short while later it broke into several smaller, white-colored objects which flew away in all directions. Claims by skeptics that this was merely a sweeping beam from a distant lighthouse are unfounded; we could see the unknown light and the lighthouse simultaneously. The latter was 35 to 40-degrees off where all of this was happening."

Sceptics have pointed out discrepancies with the 2010 statement and a tape recording Halt made at the time.

Nonetheless, Orford Ness lighthouse had by then gained international fame.

The UK government has released some documents about the case, but the US government remains silent. Meanwhile, the Forestry Commission has marked an UFO Trail for walkers, which includes locations such as the small clearing where the object allegedly landed. A large triangular shaped metal information board at the start gives a basic account of the alleged incident.

The lighthouse is sited on a 13-mile long sand and shingle spit which runs parallel to the coast, from which it is divided by the estuary of the Rivers Alde and Ore.

By itself it was a major hazard to shipping, but the swift tides, banks and shoals made conditions even more treacherous.

On the night of October 28 1627, 32 ships including many Tyneside colliers were cast up on Orford Ness with hardly any survivors.

As a result, the bailiffs of Aldeburgh raised a petition to Trinity House for a lighthouse.

Sir John Meldrum, who owned the Winterton lights described in Chapter 12, submitted a petition to Charles I, to build a pair of temporary lights between Sizewell Bank and Aldeburgh Napes.

His lease of Orford Ness for 50 years was confirmed in February 1637. As stated previously, he then sold the lease to Alderman Gerard Gore, along with that of the Winterton lights.

He obtained permission from Charles II to build two timber towers 60 yards apart to indicate a safe passage through the narrow gap between the Sizewell Bank and Aldeburgh Napes. He built them on the furthest seaward point of Orford Ness, the high light being lit by coal and the low light by candle, Mariners had to line them up to see the safe passage available.

At one stage Gore allowed the widow of a lighthouse keeper to take over his duties, but became dissatisfied with her performance and removed her.

The next owner, Sir Edward Turnour, later Lord Chief Baron of the Exchequer, bought the land on which the lighthouse stood and also a large area of Lantern Marshes to provide access.

Opposite: *Orford Ness lighthouse as seen from the air – or from an alien spacecraft?* TRINITY HOUSE

*The last Orford Ness Front Light
before it fell into the sea.* MIKE
MILLICHAMP COLLECTION

His son Edward became owner on his death in 1676, but failed to adequately maintain the light, prompting many complaints from seafarers, and a successful challenge to his continuance of the lease when it expired in 1720.

Reconciled to the fact he would lose the lease when the current one expired, the heavily-in-debt Turnour spent even less of his time maintaining his Orford lights.

In January 1690, his junior lighthouse keeper was carried off by the press gang.

That year, coastal erosion led to his lower light being moved back by 30 yards, but a year later it was washed away altogether. Turnour replaced it with one of identical design, but it too was washed away in 1709, and again replaced.

On 23 June 1707, during's Britain war with Napoleonic France, the lighthouses were attacked by a French privateer. The lantern was severely damaged and goods including the keeper's bed were stolen.

Turnour's lease expired in 1720, and was taken over by Henry Grey, whose men had to wrestle the keys from Turnour's staff in a scuffle outside the higher light on the event of April 12. Turnour began legal proceedings for trespass, but died in 1721 before they came to court.

Grey replaced the wooden towers with brick alternatives. The lower one had to be replaced in 1732 after also being washed away.

John Griffin Griffin, Lord Braybrooke of Audley End near Saffron Walden, whose family had inherited Grey's estates, became their owner in 1762.

On the night of 31 October 1789, a huge storm ravaged the coast of East Anglia, scouring away shingle leaving the low lighthouse on the water's edge.

In 1792, Braybrooke had a new 89ft brick high tower built much further back. Designed by the architect William Wilkins, the son of a Norwich plasterer and stucco worker, it became the Great Ore High Light, and is the Ordford Ness lighthouse we have today.

Fourteen oil lamps were placed behind silver-plated reflectors, and the first light was shone on 14 October 1793.

Its predecessor became the small or lower light, and the one it replaced was left to its inevitable fate.

The 1836 Act of Parliament saw Trinity House compulsorily purchase Orford Ness lighthouse from the third Lord Braybrooke for £13,414 and take it over from New Year's Day the following year.

Immediately, improvements were made in the locality. A floating light was positioned at Shipwash Sands eight miles south east of the lighthouse.

In 1838, a new French lens was fitted to the lower light, while the higher light received two more burners, making 16 in total.

The first submarine telegraph cable from England to The Netherlands was laid over the 115 miles between Orford Ness and Scheveningen in May and early June 1853. The cable laying was carried out by R. S. Newall & Company under contract from the Electric & International Telegraph Company, with the telegraph equipment housed in the lighthouse. The feat was considered remarkable in view of an horrendous gale which hampered progress of the vessels involved.

The lower lighthouse succumbed to beach erosion in 1887 following a huge shingle-shifting storm and this time was never replaced. In all, there had been five lower towers, two which burned down and three lost to the waves. On exceptionally-low spring tides, the brick foundations can sometimes be seen.

Trinity House decided not to replace it, and as we have seen, instead built a replacement at Southwold to the north.

Lonely Orford Ness lighthouse on its shingle spit. DAVID MERRITT*

Major modifications to Orford Ness lighthouse were made in the 1860s, when new Fresnel prisms were introduced., with the latest types of reflective mirrors, while in 1888, the light was made occulting and red and green shades were fitted to form sector lights.

In 1914, the present revolving lens was installed. Under the arrangement, three vertical circular lenses are mounted on a circular platform which floats on a trough of mercury. The lens revolves around the lamp at a speed which appears as a flash every five seconds.

At the same time, another light was brought into operation half way up the tower. This sector light is a fixed light showing through red and green windows facing south east and a red window facing north east.

These and other lenses subsequently fitted over the years were installed by the firm of Stone-Chance.

Orford Ness was now classed as a rock station because of its remote position on the shingle spit, which needed to be accessed by boat from Orford.

The light was converted to incandescent gas during Edwardian times.

During World War One, the remoteness of Orford led to it being chosen for secret military activities, such as the testing of weaponry.

The site was chosen as the location for the Orford Ness Beacon, a very early experiment in long-range radio navigation set up in 1929. In the thirties, Orford Ness was the site of the first radar experiments developed by Robert Watson-Watt who developed the Chain Home radar system in time for the Battle of Britain.

In 1934, Orford Ness was made a restricted area, housing an experimental bombing range.

Due to tightening security and safety concerns, the keepers' families were moved out in 1936.

During both world wars, the light was extinguished apart from times when the Royal Navy needed to guide a coastal convoy.

The tower served as a useful marker for incoming bombers returning from raids over Nazi Germany.

In echoes of the earlier Dudgeon lightship incident, the lighthouse was machine-gunned by the Luftwaffe, and in 1940 an Italian aircraft crashed a few yards to the north. A V1 doodlebug flying bomb exploded by the lighthouse in 1944.

In 1959 the lighthouse was converted to electric power, and the two keeper's cottages either side of the tower were demolished.

The last keepers to operate on the site left on 20 September 1965, their work was replaced by monthly visits to check the equipment. In 1991, a Logic Control Unit was installed, guaranteeing failure to be impossible. However, faulty lighting conductors did cause a rare failure in 2000. The most recent form of illumination is a one-kilowatt 240V Mercury Vapour Discharge lamp.

The Atomic Weapons Research Establishment, founded in 1950, subsequently developed a base at Orford, used for environmental testing, and in the late sixties, Cobra Mist, an experimental Anglo-American military over-the-horizon radar facility, was built.

It closed in 1973, and the site and building were reused for the Orford Ness transmitting station, famous for broadcasting BBC World Service in English to continental Europe on 648 kHz medium wave from September 1982 until March 2011. The station became disused in May 2012.

Orford Ness the locality is now owned by the National Trust and while it is open to the public, access is strictly controlled, both to protect the fragile wildlife habitats and visitors from unexploded bombs. Access is available only by the National Trust ferry from Orford Quay on listed open days.

There are many ruined buildings on the shingle spit, and it seems that at best, Orford Ness lighthouse will now join them.

Because of the rate of coastal erosion, in 2004 Trinity House expressed fears that the lighthouse with its distinctive red and white striped bands would not survive another five years.

In April 2009, a representative addressed the Alde and Ore Association's river defence committee and said it was considering either building a new lighthouse or moving the existing one at a cost of £4.5 million.

The following January, Trinity House announced that the light would be discontinued, as GPS systems could do the job instead. Association members issued a statement issuing fears about the dire consequences should satellite systems fail.

The National Trust wants to take over the lighthouse once it is turned off for good, but only after Trinity House removes any hazardous materials. It is proposed to remove parts of it for exhibition elsewhere and then leave the tower to the mercy of the unstoppable sea, meaning the end to one of East Anglia's most distinctive landmarks of all.

We do not know if the Daleks, Cybermen or any other alien life visited Rendlesham Forest, but a lighthouse did feature in a 1977 Dr Who story, 'Horror of Fang Rock', in which he encountered the Rutans. If aliens did show up in Suffolk in 1980, maybe Orford Ness lighthouse was being inadvertently used as East Anglia's first intergalactic navigational beacon. On the other hand, if the mysterious visitors were indeed from our future, I hope they had inherited a copy of this book to help guide them.

A famous British Railways poster featuring Orford Ness lighthouse.
ROBIN JONES COLLECTION

ORFORD NESS near WOODBRIDGE, SUFFOLK

EAST COAST LANDMARKS

SEE BRITAIN BY TRAIN

CHAPTER EIGHTEEN
LANDGUARD POINT

LANDGUARD POINT lies on the northern bank of the River Orwell in Essex, close to the port of Felixstowe. Harwich Harbour, at the mouth of the river, has always been the safest haven for large ships between the Thames and Humber.

However, the Orwell, Stour and Deben formed perfect inland highways for both traders and raiders.

Landguard Fort oversaw the navigable channel of the Orwell. It had its origins in a pair of blockhouses built by Henry VII in 1543.

A new fort was built in 1628, and a brick wall added in 1666 on the orders of Charles II. The following year, during the second Dutch War, 1,500 Dutch marines landed at Cobbolds Point. Commanded by turncoat Colonel Thomas Dolman, an English officer who had served under Oliver Cromwell and had changed sides, the marines attacked the fort from the land. The Duke of York and Albany's Maritime Regiment of Foot (the first English marines), repulsed the Dutch assault: the fort has since been able to boast that it is the only one in Britain to have repelled a full-scale invasion attempt. In the centuries that followed, the fort was enlarged and improved several times.

What concerns us here is the fact that from 1848, a light was shown from the fort from 1848 to guide the way for shipping to enter the port of Harwich.

It sufficed until a full-blown lighthouse was built 390 yards from the tip of Landguard Point.

The white-painted wooden-framed structure on legs stood 38ft high, with an adjacent keeper's chalet.

The fort light was discontinued when the new lighthouse came into operation on 10 June 1861.

The white light was said to have been occulting every 10 seconds.

The lantern with a dioptric lens was 33ft above sea level and the light could be seen for 10 miles.

An Edwardian hand-coloured postcard of Landguard Point lighthouse. MIKE MILLCHAMP COLLECTION

Opposite: *Close-up of the wooden tower.* MIKE MILLCHAMP COLLECTION

It had a sector which showed red from Andrews Buoy to the Beach End Buoy. The light was amended in 1868, 1878 and 1896.

The lighthouse was destroyed by fire on 6 April 1925 and there is nothing on the site to indicate that it was ever there

It was not replaced, as again, the channels had altered their course and it would have been redundant in any case.

No trace of it exists today and given the changing currents which alter the channels, then there is no requirement for a replacement light.

Landguard Fort's purpose ended in 1956 when the Coastal Artillery was disbanded.

Neglected, it was left to fall derelict until the 1980s when local moves to save it were begun.

It passed into the hands of English Heritage, and has been maintained and opened to the public on their behalf by the Landguard Fort Trust.

Darell's Batteries at Landguard Fort date from 1901, after it had ceased to be a navigational aid. ANDREW GALLOWAY*

CHAPTER NINETEEN
THE PIRATE LIGHTSHIP

EVERY COASTLINE has its fair share of pirate stories, but this one concerns radio broadcasts rather than parrots and pieces of eight.

Our story here relates to Trinity House lightship LV18, the last manned Trinity House lightvessel in service, which in 2011 was moored at Ha'Penny Pier in Harwich Quay after being turned into a tourist attraction.

Built by Philip & Son of Dartmouth and launched on 21 July 1958, she first served on St Gowan station in Wales. She was withdrawn from service in 1995 and two years later sold to Sea Containers Ltd to become a centrepiece of a proposed development at House Creek in Harwich which never got off the ground.

In 1999, the lightship went to sea again. It was for licensed offshore broadcasting as Radio North Sea International, Radio Caroline and Radio Mi Amigo. It was also used to broadcast

Radio Sunshine – the pirate ship of the film The Boat That Rocked *back home in Harwich.* MARIA FOWLER

Above: *The rear of LV87 berthed in the marina at Levington.* ROBIN JONES

Opposite: *Cromer station veteran lightship LV87 is today a yacht club headquarters near Ipswich.* ROBIN JONES

transmissions as 'Pirate' BBC Essex, in 2004 and 2007.

The second occasion saw broadcasting from the lightship last for a week to mark the 40th anniversary of the Marine Offences Act, which made pirate radio stations illegal before BBC1 launched its own legal pop music station, Radio 1. It employed many of the disc jockeys who had previously been involved with pirate stations off the coast of Harwich such as the legendary first-time-round Caroline and Radio London.

To mark the anniversary, several of them including Johnny Walker, Dave Cash, Roger Day, Keith Skues and Emperor Rosco made a comeback to the sea waves as well as the air variety to relieve past times. They lived abroad LV18 for a week, and the stunt attracted many visitors to the port.

In 2001, Sea Containers sold LV18 to the Pharos Trust for a nominal £1. The trust was set up to restore it at Harwich.

LV18 attained stardom in spring 2008 when it was towed to Portland in Dorset to star in a hit movie about the sixties pirate radio stations, *The Boat That Rocked*. It was specially painted in red and yellow 'Radio Sunshine' pirate station livery for the film, and returned to Harwich in that temporary condition.

Emmy and BAFTA award-winning filmmaker Richard Curtis wrote the script. His previous projects ranged from *Four Weddings and a Funeral, Notting Hill, Bridget Jones's Diary* and *Love Actually* to *Mr Bean* and *Blackadder*.

The film starred Rhys Ifans, Kenneth Brannagh, Bill Nighy and Philip Seymour Hoffman alongside and on board LV18.

BBC Essex again broadcast from LV18 during Easter 2009, before a two-year restoration project began. Meanwhile, Tendring District and Essex County councils obtained £220,000 in grant aid funding from the Haven Gateway Partnership to create a mooring for the vessel. There, it will serve as a museum portraying the history of lightships and their part in guiding sailors around the British coastline.

The River Orwell had by then for several years been a happy resting place for another lightship.

Upstream on the north bank at Levington, at Suffolk Yacht Harbour, a marina, with 550 berths, LV87 has a permanent mooring and is now the clubhouse of the Haven Ports Yacht Club.

LV87 was built for Trinity House in 1932 by A.J. Inglis of Pointhouse, Glasgow, and served on the East Goodwin, Mid-Barrow, and Cromer stations.

She was decommissioned in 1973 and sold to the yacht club, but the light tower was removed for use on the Inner Dowsing light platform. However, the club was able to buy the light tower of LV88, although it was not identical.

Opposite, left: *LV18 in Harwich Quay during Lifeboat Fun Day 2011.* MARIA FOWLER

Opposite, right: *The tower on LV87 came from LV88.* ROBIN JONES

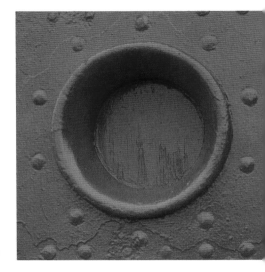

CHAPTER TWENTY

HARWICH LITTLE AND LARGE

Harwich owes so much of its prosperity to the fact it provided the only safe deepwater anchorages between the Humber and the Thames, thanks to its position on the estuaries of the Stour and Orwell.

It is one of the Haven Ports, the others being Ipswich and Felixstowe.

The town's name means 'military settlement' and is derived from the Old English 'here-wic'. Indeed, its position has given it a huge military significance over the centuries. It was heavily fortified as a naval base in 1657, and on 11 November 1688, when William of Orange was invited to take the English throne from the unpopular James II, he planned to bring his invasion fleet to Harwich, but bad weather led to him landing at Torbay instead.

John Constable's masterpiece 'Harwich Lighthouse' which depicts the old wooden Low lighthouse.

Opposite: *Harwich High lighthouse is now a museum of radio and television.* DAVID WHITTLE

Opposite: Harwich Low Lighthouse is today used as the town's maritime museum. DAVID WHITTLE

In 1722, Daniel Defoe remarked on the "vast extent of the fort and harbour."

Harwich received its charter in 1238, although it may date back to Roman times. Much of the older town which includes medieval buildings and streets is now a conservation area.

Two lighthouses were first established in Harwich by 1665, working as a pair to lead ships around Landguard Point into Harwich Harbour. They were recorded in Samuel Pepy's Diary on 3 January that year.

It was said that the church tower originally showed a light, later replaced by a wooden tower, while a coal fire was lit over the town gate as a lantern.

The Low lighthouse was immortalised by the artist John Constable in his painting of 'Harwich Lighthouse', of which he produced three versions with only slight differences. He based them on sketches made between 1815-17 and one of them was displayed at the Royal Academy in 1802.

At the time, both lighthouses were leased by Constable's friend and patron, Major-General Slater-Rebow of Wivenhoe Park.

The pair provided Rebow with an income from tolls from passing ships, charging a penny per ton light duties on all cargoes coming into Harwich, but in return he was required to maintain them. He was granted a new lease in 1817 on condition that he rebuilt them.

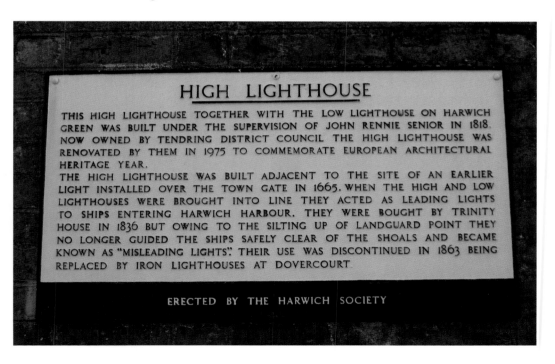

HIGH LIGHTHOUSE

THIS HIGH LIGHTHOUSE TOGETHER WITH THE LOW LIGHTHOUSE ON HARWICH GREEN WAS BUILT UNDER THE SUPERVISION OF JOHN RENNIE SENIOR IN 1818. NOW OWNED BY TENDRING DISTRICT COUNCIL THE HIGH LIGHTHOUSE WAS RENOVATED BY THEM IN 1975 TO COMMEMORATE EUROPEAN ARCHITECTURAL HERITAGE YEAR.
THE HIGH LIGHTHOUSE WAS BUILT ADJACENT TO THE SITE OF AN EARLIER LIGHT INSTALLED OVER THE TOWN GATE IN 1665. WHEN THE HIGH AND LOW LIGHTHOUSES WERE BROUGHT INTO LINE THEY ACTED AS LEADING LIGHTS TO SHIPS ENTERING HARWICH HARBOUR. THEY WERE BOUGHT BY TRINITY HOUSE IN 1836 BUT OWING TO THE SILTING UP OF LANDGUARD POINT THEY NO LONGER GUIDED THE SHIPS SAFELY CLEAR OF THE SHOALS AND BECAME KNOWN AS "MISLEADING LIGHTS". THEIR USE WAS DISCONTINUED IN 1863 BEING REPLACED BY IRON LIGHTHOUSES AT DOVERCOURT.

ERECTED BY THE HARWICH SOCIETY

A plaque attached to the High lighthouse. DAVID WHITTLE

Above: *It is said that early navigational lights were shown from the tower of Harwich's church.* MARTIN PETTITT*

Left: *Harwich High lighthouse.* HARWICH SOCIETY

As a result, Harwich was left with a "little and large" pair of unalike twins 150 yards apart.

The new pair were built by the pioneering Scottish canal, bridge and dock builder John Rennie Senior, later responsible for London Bridge.

Now Grade I listed, the High lighthouse in West Street in the middle of the town, the Range Rear light, is a 90ft nine-sided tower built from grey gault brick while the Low lighthouse is a 45ft ten-sided brick tower, while the ground storey has a projecting canopy as a public shelter.

Each was built nine feet to the south west of the sites of the original lights. At the High lighthouse, the light was shown through a top-storey window. Ships had to line them up to ensure they were on the correct course.

In 1836, Rebow sold the pair to Trinity House, but they became useless when the channel around Landguard Point silted up, and they were disused from 1863. For many years before, as the channel deteriorated, they were known as "misleading lights". As we will see in the next chapter, they were replaced by a pair of iron lighthouses at nearby Dovercourt Bay.

In 1909, both were bought by Harwich Borough Council, and the High lighthouse became a private residence for many years.

The council carried out some restoration of the High lighthouse in 1974 to mark European Architectural Heritage Year, but it remained empty for the next 17 years as no further use could be found for it. The National Vintage Wireless and Television Museum Trust leased the High lighthouse from Tendring District Council 1991. The trust transferred its exhibits from its previous museum at Dedham and opened the lighthouse to visitors in 1995.

The use of the building for such a purpose was certainly appropriate, for Guglielmo Marconi's first wireless school was sited at nearby Frinton-on-Sea. Before his first successful radio transmission across the Atlantic, experimental broadcasts were made from nearby Dovercourt, next to the Cliff Hotel.

The museum is laid out in a chronological series of period 'room sets' on each floor of the lighthouse, each decorated in the style of the period, showing the evolution of radio and television in the twentieth century.

When Trinity House passed over the Low lighthouse to the council, it retained the right to use it if ever the need arose. In the late sixties and seventies, it saw a second lease of life as a pilot station.

It was subsequently used as a pilot signal station from 1970-74. Afterwards, it reverted to Tendring District Council when the new pilot station was completed.

The Harwich Society took over the Low lighthouse in Harbour Crescent and opened it as the Harwich Maritime Museum in 1980. It is today a popular tourist attraction, containing everything from photographs and paintings to ships in bottles and lighthouse bulbs. It offers a sweeping view of the harbour from the top floor, and an active radio link to harbour control serves as a reminder of its years as a pilot signal station.

Early twentieth-century postcard view of Harwich High Light, by then long since disused. ROBIN JONES COLLECTION

CHAPTER TWENTY ONE
THE DOVERCOURT RANGE LIGHTS

DOVERCOURT IS THE beach resort for neighbouring Harwich, used at the setting for BBC1's comedy series Hi De Hi! in the eighties, when Warner's Holiday Camp was turned into Maplin's.

It also contains a pair of lighthouses which replaced the two at Harwich in 1863.

These leading lights were built on the beach for the purpose of guiding ships around Landguard Point.

The Low or Range Front lighthouse stands 27ft high just offshore and has a hexagonal lantern, watch room, and gallery supported by four cast iron screwpile legs. For an explanation of screwpile technology in lighthouse design, please refer to chapter 26.

Waves smash against the sea front near the High lighthouse in this vintage hand-coloured view. ROBIN JONES COLLECTION

Rough Sea. Dovercourt Bay.

Opposite: *Dovercourt's High and Low lighthouses lined up together.* DAVID WHITTLE

The sun rises behind Dovercourt Low lighthouse. ANDREW STAWARZ*

View of both lighthouses from the south west. R WENDLAND*

The High or Range Rear lighthouse is built on the beach next to the promenade and has a 45 ft hexagonal lantern, watch room and gallery supported on six cast iron legs. The towers and roofs of both are painted black with white lanterns.

Equipped with powerful gas lamps, they lasted in service for little more than half a century, for the channel changed its course again, and in 1917 they were declared redundant. In 1922

they were sold to Harwich Town Council on condition that they would be dismantled if they became unsafe.

Much-loved landmarks that are unique in their design, they were restored between 1983-88 by the High Stewards Lighthouse Appeal and have listed building status.

The deep-water channel is now marked by buoys.

CHAPTER TWENTY TWO
TRINITY HOUSE OPERATIONS AND PLANNING CENTRE

THE DAYS OF MANNED lighthouses in Britain are now long since over. All of the country's lighthouses have been automatic since November 1988, when the last keepers left North Foreland in Kent.

While automation dates back to 1910, when Swedish inventor Nils Gustaf Dalén produced a sun valve which in daylight cut the supply to lighthouses supplied by acetylene gas (he was awarded the Nobel Prize for Physics as a result two years later), it began in earnest in the early Eighties when lantern-top helipads were installed at remote rock lighthouses, allowing technicians to be quickly brought in during breakdowns. They eliminated the need for residential staff.

Also, strides made in remote control technology allowed all lighthouses and lightships in England and Wales to be controlled from one point, the Trinity House Operations and Planning Centre in Harwich.

From the control centre, all navigational aids are monitored 24 hours a day, 365 days a year.

Harwich has had a Trinity House depot since 1812. The main depot was moved from Blackwall in London to Harwich in 1940, and in 2005 a new office block between West Street and the Quay was built to house the operational headquarters.

At the same time, a new Buoy Yard was built in George Street, Harwich. In the adjacent harbour, lightships being serviced by the depot can frequently be seen.

Tours of both the Corporation's headquarters in Trinity Square in London next to Tower Hill and the operational headquarters in Harwich including the control centre are available.

The Corporation of Trinity House of Deptford Strond, to give the organisation its full title, was founded in 1514, when Henry VIII granted a Royal Charter in the name of "The Master, Wardens, and Assistants of the Guild, Fraternity, or Brotherhood of the most glorious and undivided Trinity, and of St Clement in the Parish of Deptford-Strond in the County of Kent."

The name derives from the church of Holy Trinity and St Clement, which stood next to the king's new dockyard at Deptford.

Trinity House is ruled by a court of 31 Elder Brethren, presided over by a Master. The first Master was Thomas Spert, captain of Henry's ill-fated flagship *Mary Rose*. The Princess Royal

The Trinity House headquarters in Harwich. TRINITY HOUSE

The control centre in Harwich monitors navigational aids around the clock.
TRINITY HOUSE

today holds the now-honorary position of Master. Previous Masters of Trinity House have included, as we saw earlier, Samuel Pepys and the Duke of Wellington.

The Elder Brethren are chosen from 300 Younger Brethren who perform the role of advisors. These are drawn from naval officers, ships' masters, harbourmasters, pilots, yachtsmen and anyone with relevant experience.

Remote control technology has eliminated the need for lighthouse keepers to spend months on duty on isolated rock stations.
TRINITY HOUSE

In earlier chapters, we saw how Trinity House jealously guarded its rights to erect lighthouses over the centuries. Today, it is the unchallenged general lighthouse authority for England, Wales and other British waters apart from Scotland, the Isle of Man and Northern Ireland. Not only does it have responsibility for the provision and maintenance of its traditional navigational aids such as 69 operational lighthouses as well as lightships and buoys but also maritime radio and satellite communication systems.

CHAPTER TWENTY THREE
THE SUNK CENTRE LIGHTSHIP

AS WE HAVE SEEN, there were many places around the coast of East Anglia where lightships were placed in order to warn sailors off sandbanks and shoals.

Until late in the twentieth century, all Trinity House lightvessels were permanently manned. It was a dangerous and highly-skilled occupation, and it could take up to 20 years to become master of a lightship.

In the 1860s, it was reported that the crew members were "very respectable" and that swearing and profane language were prohibited. Furthermore, every man was provided with a bible and a library of books.

Supply ships arrived once a month to deliver provisions and relieve crews.

At the start of the twentieth century, lightships had 11-strong crews, with a master and six ratings on duty at any one time.

Lightships have to be towed to and from their position as they have no propulsion of their own.

In the Seventies, Trinity House embarked on a scheme to replace its lightships with Large Automatic Navigation Buoys or LANBYs. By doing so, it could cut the annual £30,000 cost of a lightship to just £3,000.

Most of the British lightships were decommissioned by the end of the Eighties, leaving just eight. All converted to unmanned operation and most use solar power.

The only one around the cost of East Anglia remaining is Sunk Centre. The name of lightships has usually been taken from the named position at which a vessel was placed, not the vessel itself.

This North Sea lightship station lies 19 miles ESE of Harwich and was established in 1802. It is part of the traffic separation scheme for ships approaching or leaving the Thames estuary.

Like all Trinity House lightships, it is painted red to be as conspicuous as possible in daylight, with the name in massive white letters along each side.

The light is shone from a square skeletal tower in the middle of the ship, and has a focal plane of 39ft. It is visible for 11 miles.

Its big claim to fame was its part in early ship to shore communication experiments. A major problem with lightships in the early decades was their inability to contact the shore:

crew members might see a ship in distress, for example, but had no way of alerting a lifeboat.

Following a series of maritime disasters, an undersea cable was run from the Sunk Centre lightship nine miles to the post office at Walton-on-the-Naze.

Due to begin in 1884, the experiment was beset by delays caused by the cable breaking time and time again.

In 1892, a Royal Commission reported on the possibility of electrical communication with lightships. Four years later, the East Goodwin lightship in Kent was used for one of Guglielmo Marconi's early experiments in radio transmission, and this paved the way for the problem to be solved. The world's first radio distress signal was transmitted by the East Goodwin lightship's radio operator on 17 March 1899.

Today, the Sunk Centre lightship also acts as a weather station.

The unmanned Sunk Centre lightship relies on solar power. It is visited only for occasional maintenance.
RENCO BEUNIS

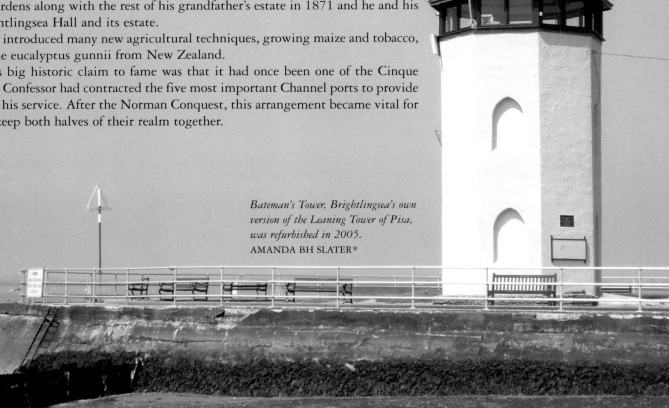

THE STORY OF THE very unusual navigation aid that is Bateman's Tower at Brightlingsea in Essex began 220 miles away in landlocked Staffordshire.

Biddulph Grange Gardens, one of the greatest survivors from the heyday of Victorian gardens, was created by owners James and Maria Bateman, and their friend Edward Cooke. James had been fascinated by orchids since he was eight, while his wife was keen on fuschias and lilies. James imported many trees and shrubs from around the world.

In the 1860s, the couple passed the gardens on to their son John and retired to Worthing.

John Bateman, born in 1839, and a graduate of Trinity College, Cambridge, served as Deputy Lieutenant for Staffordshire and chairman of the local magistrates.

He sold the gardens along with the rest of his grandfather's estate in 1871 and he and his wife bought Brightlingsea Hall and its estate.

Once there, he introduced many new agricultural techniques, growing maize and tobacco, and introduced the eucalyptus gunnii from New Zealand.

Brightlingsea's big historic claim to fame was that it had once been one of the Cinque Ports. Edward the Confessor had contracted the five most important Channel ports to provide ships and men for his service. After the Norman Conquest, this arrangement became vital for the monarchs to keep both halves of their realm together.

Bateman's Tower, Brightlingsea's own version of the Leaning Tower of Pisa, was refurbished in 2005.
AMANDA BH SLATER*

Sunset over Bateman's Tower, which was built as a folly and not a true lighthouse. ADRIAN ESPIN

Normandy was lost to the English throne in 1205, and afterwards, the Cinque Ports became England's first line of defence against the French, their collective fleet a forerunner of the Royal Navy.

All but one of the Confederation of the Cinque Ports was in Sussex or Kent, apart from Brightlingsea.

The role eventually became purely ceremonial, and the Cinque Port Liberty was revived at Brightlingsea in the 1880s. John Bateman became the port's first Deputy and held the office from 1887-91 and again in 1899 and 1903. He presented the town with the Deputy's badge and chain of office which is still worn today.

A great benefactor to the town, where he was known as the 'Old Squire,' he served as Deputy Lieutenant for Essex, a local and county councillor and a magistrate.

John married his wife Jessie Caroline Bootle Wilbraham, sister of the Earl of Latham, in 1865. They had one daughter, Agnes, who in her teenage years became ill through tuberculosis.

In 1883, he built a 33ft tower for her at Westmarsh Point at the entrance to Brightlingsea Creek on the River Colne. A type of folly, the octagonal masonry tower with observation room and a conical roof bore some resemblance to a lighthouse but was not intended as such, and is often mistaken for a Martello tower, the castle-like fortifications around the coast of south-east England built as a defensive chain during the Napoleonic Wars.

John Bateman was also said to have used it as a bathing hut for his family and guests, or as a wildflower's retreat, for when it was built, it was surrounded by marshes.

The tower leans out of true. A story runs that it was built on bundles of faggots to provide a foundation in the marshland. It has been claimed to move towards the perpendicular with each rising tide. John Bateman died at Brightlingsea Hall on 12 October 1910.

The roof of the tower was removed during World War II, when the tower was used by the Royal Observer Corps.

Bateman's Tower towers above Brightlingsea's beach huts.
DAN DAVISON*

There was outrage in Brightlingsea in 1974 when Tendring District Council proposed knocking it down, fearing that one day it might lean too far and topple over. Waving aside protestors from the town council, tenders for the demolition were invited, but one of the demolition firms instead offered to take over the lease on the tower from the Colne Yacht Club, make it safe, refurbish it and then lease it back at a nominal rent. In 2005, the tower was restored with a copper-clad replica of the original roof installed and the interior and exterior refurbished, in a Heritage Lottery Fund-backed project carried out by the Colne Yacht Club. The public were allowed in for guided tours on 7 May 2005.

Not only does it act as a daymark for vessels in the Colne estuary, but at some stage a large sodium vertical light was added as a privately-maintained navigational aid, showing a continuous yellow light with a focal plane of 39ft.

Around 2007, the light was replaced with a smaller version, flashing three times every 20 seconds.

The yacht club, Colne Smack Preservation Society and other sailing organisations today use the tower for the administration of sailing races in the Colne estuary.

CHAPTER TWENTY FIVE
NAZE TOWER

THE NAZE TOWER at Walton-on-the-Naze is known locally as 'The Landmark' and is exactly that.

The Grade II* listed structure was built in 1721 by Trinity House as a daymark for shipping, long before lighthouses became commonplace.

Standing 86ft tall and totally unmistakeable, the Hanoverian tower was designed as a marker for ships approaching Harwich Harbour, and still performs this function today It is said to be the only building of its type and era in Britain and possibly the world.

The term 'Naze' derives from the same Old English word 'næss' as 'ness' as in Winterton Ness or Orford Ness, meaning a headland or promontory.

The Naze, which lies to the north of the town of Walton, is renowned for its natural habitats and fossils, any of which are exposed through coastal erosion. The cliffs are designated a Site of Special Scientific Interest because of their rich fossil content.

The clifftop was originally farmland, and later became a privately-owned golf course. The local council bought it in 1967 and turned it into public open space.

The dense brambles and hawthorn provide a haven for hundreds of species of animals and insects and an important area for migrating birds, while nearby Hamford Water, another SSSI, is a breeding ground for ginger-coloured seals, their fur acquiring this colour from the estuarine mud.

In the early twentieth century, radio masts were installed at the top of the tower during experiments in long-range transmission.

During World War Two, the tower and surrounding area was requisitioned as a lookout location.

Following its purchase by a local resident, the tower has been refurbished and in 2004 was opened as a visitor centre with tea room and six-storey gallery showcasing and selling the works of East Anglian artists.

Visitors can climb all 111 steps of the Victorian spiral staircase to the roof vieweing platform for unrivalled 360 degrees views over the Essex and Suffolk coast and Kent can be seen on a clear day.

It also contains a museum with exhibits about the tower, and the ecology and geology of the Naze.

Naze Tower has been claimed to be the only building of its type in the world.
ROBIN JONES

The tower may be protected in law as a listed building, but such statutes have no control over the sea. When built, the town was a quarter of a mile from the sea, and now it is just 60 yards away. Every year, around seven feet of cliff crash into the sea.

Within 20 years, the tower could easily go the way of the Orford Ness and Happisburgh low lights and succumb to the power of the waves. Dotted on the beach are the ruins of World War Two clifftop pillboxes that have met the same fate.

The Naze Protection Society has been formed to campaign for erosion controls and has a charity fundraising shop in the town. Protection measures installed along the coast here include a sea wall, rock armour groynes and drainage, while millions of tons of sand have been added to the beach to replenish it and halt cliff erosion.

The Naze Tower owner along with the society, Essex Wildlife Trust, Tendring District Council, Essex County Council, Frinton and Walton Town Council and local landowners are working together to secure the future for the Naze as a nationally-important area for heritage and wildlife. Crag Walk, a 130-yard public access and viewing platform sited along the beach in front of the southern end of the Naze cliffs, is a first step in a longer-term aim to preserve both the public open space and the tower.

The Hanoverian Naze Tower was built as a daymark to serve Harwich shipping. ROBIN JONES

CHAPTER TWENTY SIX
GUNFLEET

SIX MILES OFF the coast of Frinton-on-Sea stands a lighthouse that has been out of action for nearly half a century.

On the north-east limit of the Port of London, Gunfleet lighthouse which marked the treacherous Gunfleet Sands is marginally inside British territorial waters.

It dates from 1850 and was built as a screwpile lighthouse based on the invention of blind Irish inventor Alexander Mitchell and designed by James Walker of Trinity House.

Gunfleet was not the world's first screwpile lighthouse: that honour went in 1838 to Maplin Sands which we will encounter later on. It is, however, the first we encounter in our journey around the coast, and therefore presents the chance to introduce the concept.

Alexander Mitchell was born in 1870 but was blind from 1802 until his death in 1868. A native of Dublin, he attended Belfast Academy where he excelled in mathematics.

In Belfast, he became a brickmaker and invented machines to speed up the job. He also invented the wrought-iron screwpile lighthouse which could be installed on shifting sandbanks and mudflats, and ended up being used all over the world. They literally comprise piles that are screwed into the sea or river bed in the same way that an ordinary screw is twisted into wood. Once the piles are secure, a platform is built on top of them, followed by living accommodation for the keepers and then the light on top.

The piles offer no resistance to waves which pass through the open spaces without rising any higher.

In many ways they superseded the straight-pile tubular skeletal tower lighthouse usually made of cast iron or wrought iron. By comparison with standard lighthouses, screwpile versions were cheaper, easier and quicker to build.

The typical screwpile lighthouse was hexagonal or octagonal. It would comprise a central pile which was set in the seabed first, before the six or eight perimeter piles were screwed in place around it.

In 1848 Mitchell became a member of the Institution of Civil Engineers and was awarded the Telford Medal after presenting a paper on his lighthouse invention.

Gunfleet lighthouse, which stands 74ft high, comprises an iron lattice structure built on seven screw piles driven into the shifting sands on the seabed.

Six of the piles form an outer hexagon and the seventh is a centre support on which is

Gunfleet lighthouse before its light was removed, as seen in an old postcard.
MIKE MILLICHAMP COLLECTION

carried hexagonal-shaped living accommodation consisting of a living room, a bedroom, a kitchen and washroom and a storeroom.

The lighthouse was painted red and displayed a revolving light every 30 seconds and could be seen for ten miles. It also had a fog warning bell.

It was decommissioned in 1921, but according to some reports, was not left unattended.

In 1974, during the last wave of offshore pirate radio stations that had largely been killed off in 1967 by the BBC's launch of Radio 1, an attempt was made to board Gunfleet and turn it into Radio Atlantis, a Flemish service, and Radio Atlantis and Radio Dolphin, an international station.

New windows were cut in the living accommodation and rooms on the upper floors built for the generator and transmitter which had been bought from the United States.

Like the mythical Atlantis, the attempt swiftly sank without a trace after the Home Office raided the lighthouse on 26 October 1974 and removed several items.

The two proponents of the radio station scheme arrived in a small dinghy on 19 December, but Home Office staff had been tipped off that supplies were to be delivered that day and followed behind in a boat of their own. The pair managed to board the lighthouse but found it surrounded by large vessels carrying Trinity House officers, Royal Marine Commandos and possibly Essex policemen. After a stand-off, the pair left, and so the likes of Slade, Gary Glitter, David Bowie, Suzi Quatro, Gloria Gaynor and Mud, chart toppers of the day, would never hit the airwaves from Gunfleet.

The lighthouse remains in use today as a weather station, and the sands are marked by a number of buoys with bells. It stands somewhat in the shadow of DONG Energy's Gunfleet Sands Offshore Wind Farm, which began generating in August 2009 and where the 48 giant masts and blades dwarf the small but very sturdy Victorian structure from afar.

Gunfleet Offshore Wind Farm is controlled from Brightlingsea and has a total capacity of 172 megawatts, enough to supply 125,000 households. DONG Energy

CHAPTER TWENTY SEVEN
FOUR ESSEX LIGHTSHIPS

DESPITE THE FACT that they have no propulsion of their own, many lightships have found second uses after being sold off by Trinity House.

The two-masted steel lightship LV16 Colne Light was built by Phillip & Son Ltd., of Dartmouth in 1954. She served at many stations around the British coast including South Goodwin where she was damaged in 1960.

She had her own helipad on board as the crews were changed by helicopter. Her light had a range of 11 miles.

She was decommissioned in 1988 and sold off privately. From 1988 until 1991, berthed in Southampton Docks, she was used by the Astrid Trust as a support ship.

LV15 Trinity amidst the Woodrolfe Creek saltings at Tollesbury near Maldon. CHELMSFORD BLUE*

LV38 Gull, *rotting away on the foreshore at Grays.* MIKE CHILDS

Having arrived in Colchester in 1991, she is now owned by Colchester Sea Cadets, and used as the group's headquarters. She is moored on King Edward Quay at Hythe, a dockside area on the Colne estuary, and named TS Colne Light.

She is maintained in tip-top condition although the group will never use the light because of fears it could interfere with air traffic.

Beached on Woodrolfe Creek at Tollesbury, on the northern bank of the Blackwater estuary, is LV15 Trinity.

Also built by Philip & Son, in 1955, she served at various stations including Scarweather in Swansea Bay. In 1988, she was sold to Fellowship Afloat, a Christian charitable trust for adventure and exploring the environment and two years later converted into a residential centre. She provides accommodation for participants in its nautical activity courses.

Both of these stand resplendent in their coats of bright red paint. The same cannot be said for two other lightships which have found Essex to be a less than happy retirement home.

Barely discernible as a lightship today is LV44, which was built by C. Hill & Sons in Bristol. Mainly used in Caernarfon Bay, she has an East Anglia pedigree having also been stationed at Newarp.

She was decommissioned by Trinity House in 1945 and sold to Erith Yacht Club. Years later, she was resold to the Pitsea Yacht Club.

She became moored in Vange Creek, Pitsea, where she was used as a clubhouse for boaters using the marina at Wat Tyler Country Park.

On a very high spring tide in 1990, LV44 was refloated and towed out of the creek to the nearby saltings, where she lies rotting away, restoration as good as impossible.

LV16 Colne Light at her mooring near Colchester. CSC

The light and mast of LV38 being taken away for future restoration. TRINITY HOUSE

The light tower on LV16, now used by Colchester Sea Cadets. CSC

Even so, she has still fared better than LV38 Gull, built in 1860. She was involved in a fatal accident while stationed at the Goodwin Sands on 18 March 1929. In fog she was rammed by the ship *City of York*, resulting in the death of Captain W. Williams of the lightship. She was repaired and refitted for many more years service before she was decommissioned and moored at Gorleston-on-Sea.

In 1947 she was bought for £750 by Thurrock Yacht Club, and towed to Grays where she was converted into the club's headquarters.

She was last used as a clubhouse in 1971, and was sold again in 1982. Believed to be the second oldest surviving lightship in the world, following years of vandalism and neglect, she was badly damaged by a fire in 2002.

Beached on the foreshore at Grays, conservationists became increasingly concerned about her rapid deterioration, especially in view of her historical significance.

The mast of the ship was removed in 2009 for restoration as a monument in its own right at Grays Riverside, and placed in storage until funding estimated at £48,000 for its restoration could be found.

However, in early October 2011, it was reported that the lightship herself had been scrapped.

CHAPTER TWENTY EIGHT
BLACKWATER SAILING CLUBS

TWO SAILING CLUBS on the estuary of the River Blackwater in Essex maintain their own modern lights.

The Blackwater Sailing Club on the north bank of the estuary at Heybridge to the east of Maldon has a light mounted on the front of its two-storey clubhouse on the waterfront.

With a focal plane of 33ft, it flashes green, 2.5 seconds on, 2.5 seconds off.

Until 2008 this was the only light to steer for on the 'corner' at Hilly Pool, but Hilly Pool port hand buoy is now lit. Before this, the exact point at which to turn into Colliers Reach was not marked at night.

The Blackwater Sailing Club premises and a close-up of the light on the front.
GUY HAWKINS

The Hallam light on top of Marconi Sailing club. DEREK GARDNER

A memorial plaque below the Marconi Club light. DEREK GARDNER

The Marconi Sailing Club on the south bank of the estuary has a light mounted on top of its two-storey clubhouse in Stansgate Road.

It is called the Hallam Light in memory of Terry Hallam, the drawing office manager at the Marconi research laboratories in Great Baddow. He was a keen cruising sailor and with the support of several other staff was instrumental in the formation of the sailing section of the Marconi Athletic and Social Club in 1952 and was elected as its first commodore. He held the office for the following two years and was elected again for 1964-66. Boaters trying to sail up the Blackwater after dark often had difficulty navigating the Stansgate Narrows and it was decided that a navigational aid was needed. After obtaining the necessary approvals it was agreed that a light be erected above the clubhouse. The light is a simple upright small street light on the top of a pole. It contains a sodium lamp and emits a yellow light and turns itself on at dusk and off at dawn. Such was Terry's contribution to the development of the sailing club and his love of cruising that it was named after him.

With a focal plane of 23ft, not only does it provide a useful marker in the river, but alerts passing craft to the presence of the club.

CHAPTER TWENTY NINE
THE NORE LIGHTSHIP

HISTORY WAS MADE at the entrance to one of the world's greatest shipping lanes in 1731.

In a bid to tackle the great hazard presented by the Nore, a sandbank stretching across the mouth of the Thames estuary at the point where it meets the North Sea, midway between Havengore Creek in Essex and Warden Point in Kent, the modern world's first lightship was stationed there. I say modern, because it is conjectured that the Romans used beacons on ships for a similar purpose.

As stated in Chapter 9, this lightship was the result of the partnership between impoverished former King's Lynn barber and ship manager Robert Hamblin and inventor David Avery. Trinity House considered the venture to be a waste of time: indeed, when a similar proposal was made in 1674, the Admiralty rejected it as the "idea of a madman."

Eventually, Trinity House saw the massive benefits to maritime safety that the lightship brought, and acquired the patent for the lightship, giving Avery lease revenues in exchange. The first Trinity House lightvessel at the Nore began operating in 1793.

The first Nore lightship, named Nore, was a small blunt-bowed wooden cargo sailing vessel with a low poop, which had a horizontal beam with lanterns lighted by candles lit at

LV86 carrying the name Nore during its time in Saint Katharine Docks next to Tower Bridge. K KRALLIS*

Above left: *A Victorian steel engraving of the Nore lightship.*

Above right: *The Nore lightship in Edwardian times.*

dusk and suspended from each end of the yardarm on the single mast.

It was sub basic technology: on stormy nights, the candles were often blown out and sometimes the lanterns were blown away altogether.

It is believed the ship had sails in case she broke adrift. The anchorage was also primitive, and in 1732 the lightship broke away from her mornings twice in three months. As a result of these problems, the use of lightships and other floating lights did not catch on as quickly as might have been expected.

In his book *Lighthouses and lightships; a descriptive and historical account of their mode of construction and organisation*, William Henry Davenport Adams states: "Other ships represent motion; this, immobility. We ask of vessels, as a rule, that they shall obey the wind and the wave; we ask of the lightship that it shall resist them. It is desired that in the most violent tides, in the midst of the angriest billows, and in situations the most exposed to the influence of the currents, it shall drag as little as possible upon its anchor. That it may at all times and in all conditions preserve the same maritime position, it is securely moored. Like a galley-slave, riveted to an iron chain, it can move neither to the right nor to the left."

Derek Grieve, the last master of Trinity House's lightship LV21 when it was based on the Newarp station off Great Yarmouth, and had the honour of taking it off station when the location was automated to be replaced by a light buoy, summed up the lightship crew member's lot: "Serving on Light Vessels was not your regular type job, neither was it like serving as a seaman on a normal ship. I once described it to someone that it was a sea journey that didn't end."

Subsequent early Nore lightvessels were wooden ships, in many cases galliots from The Netherlands. These were small one or two-masted ketch-like ships, with a rounded bow and stern transom and lateral stabilisers. They were used mainly for merchant trading in the Dutch Republic and in Germany, and were seen as eminently suitable for conversion to lightships.

However, by the end of the nineteenth century, a bigger ship with a distinctive revolving light was used.

The Nore lightship became a major landmark and was used as a major gathering point for the Royal Navy as well as other shipping. Until 1964, the sandbank marked the eastern limit of the Port of London Authority.

In May and June 1797, the Nore became the scene of a famous mutiny by Royal Navy sailors.

Following a successful similar mutiny against poor pay and conditions at Spithead near Portsmouth, the crew of HMS *Sandwich* seized the ship on 12 May. A total of 27 other ships joined in, with *Sandwich*, considered to be one of the worst in terms of its squalid and overcrowded conditions, becoming its flagship.

Although he did not help organise the revolt, sailor Richard Parker was elected President of the Delegates of the Fleet by his shipmates.

Parker was regarded as an intelligent man, although he had previously been court martialled and discharged from the Navy for insubordination.

Still smarting from the Spithead mutiny, the Admiralty was not so eager to give in to the demands of the mutineers which were formally presented on 20 May, and merely offered the participants a pardon. What particularly angered the Admiralty was a demand that the King should dissolve Parliament and make immediate peace with revolutionary France.

Parker tried to hold the mutiny together, but several other ships that had taken part slipped away, despite being fired on by the mutineers.

At first, the mutineers blockaded the Port of London, but later agreed to let merchant ships pass, possibly as an attempt to win favour amongst civilians.

Parker was arrested and swiftly convicted of treason and piracy. He and 28 other leaders were hanged from the yardarm of HMS *Sandwich* while other participants were flogged, jailed or transported to Australia.

A lightship carrying the name *Nore* can be seen at Port Werburgh Marina at Hoo near Rochester where she is used as a residential ship. Built in 1931 by J. Samuel White of Cowes in the Isle of Wight, she became Trinity House LV86, and was based at several stations, including the Nore, Cork off Harwich and Blackwall, according to the National Historic Ships Unit.

She was fitted with a dioptric electric fixed lantern and had three Crossley diesel generators for powering the lantern and two Reval air compressors for driving the reed foghorn. Decommissioned in 1974, she was sold to the Taylor Woodrow Maritime Heritage Site at London's St Katherine's Dock and became an office for a yacht broker. She was repainted and given the name *Nore* at this time. She sold to its present owner in 1996. Since 2006, the spot where the Nore lightships anchored is marked by Sea Reach No.1 Buoy.

The Nore *lightship (right) as depicted in a sketch of 1859.*

CHAPTER THIRTY

THE MAPLIN AND CHAPMAN SCREWPILES

Maplin Sands, the world's first screwpile lighthouse. MIKE MILLICHAMP COLLLECTION

ON ONE HAND, Maplin Sands are as desolate as it gets. On the other, these mudflats on the northern bank of the Thames estuary are teeming with wildlife.

It is not just that people might not want to visit this quagmire, but for much of it, and adjoining Foulness Island, they are banned from doing so. Since 1915, Foulness has been a military testing ground: 'ordinary' people (the island population is around 200) still live in the main village of Churchend, but visitors have to be invited by residents, and the general public may enter the island for just four hours on one Sunday a month in the summer months. You can sign in at the gatehouse at Great Wakering and obtain a permit for a one-car trip along the military road, but only to the island heritage centre in the old schoolhouse in Churchend for the purpose of inspecting the exhaustive collection of local history artefacts.

There is a public road which can be used when the Shoeburyness firing ranges are not in operation, but do not even think of trying it. A public right of way known as the Broomway, at low tide only crosses it at Maplin Sands.

In 1973, an Act of Parliament authorised the construction of a third London Airport on Foulness and Maplin Sands. The scheme was later dropped – partly because of the fowls that give their name to Foulness, the 'ness' meaning a promontory. It was feared that huge flocks of birds would cause a danger to jet engines.

HMS *Beagle*, the ship that took Charles Darwin on his landmark voyage of discovery, is believed to have ended its days on Foulness as a static coastguard watch vessel blocking one of the channels in a bid to curb smuggling. It was scrapped around 1870.

As stated earlier, the world's first lighthouse built to Alexander Mitchell's screwpile concept was designed by James Walker, Trinity House's consultant lighthouse engineer, and erected on Maplin Sands in 1838.

It was a 69ft high iron lattice structure built on nine screw piles driven 22ft into the mudflats on the south-eastern edge of the sands north of Shoeburyness. Eight of the piles formed an outer octagon, with the ninth acting as a centre support.

On top was installed a wooden octagonal building consisting of a living room, a bedroom, kitchen, washroom and storeroom. The bedroom housed three bunks, for the principal keeper

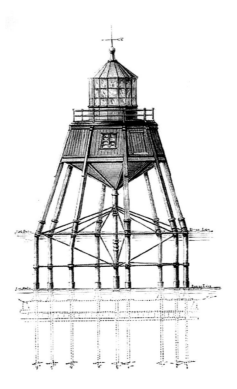

and his two assistants.

Painted bright red, the lighthouse displayed a fixed light at a height of 36ft and could be seen for ten miles. Its purpose was to warn ships off the shallow mudflats. A fog warning bell was attached to one side of the lantern gallery, with a flagpole on the other.

The strong estuarine undercurrents eventually undermined the lighthouse. Trinity House posted a notice to mariners on 26 August 1931 informing them that the light, bell and telephone communication would be closed down while the stability of the lighthouse was investigated.

However, its revolutionary screwpile technology proved useless when in 1932 it was finally swept away, never to be rebuilt.

Two very basic automatic lighthouses, mild steel lattice structures, mark the sands today.

Named Blacktail East and Blacktail West, they were positioned in 1968. Standing 42ft high, the basic navigational light on the top of each can be seen for six miles.

At one time powered by experimental wind generators, they were converted to solar power in 1996.

A similar screwpile lighthouse was erected further upstream at Canvey Island in 1851, also

Above left: *Sketch of the Maplin Sands lighthouse.* ILLUSTRATED LONDON NEWS

Above centre: *Blueprint of the Maplin Sands lighthouse.* ROBIN JONES COLLECTION

Above right: *A monument to the Maplin Sands lighthouse has been erected outside the Star Inn in the yachting haven of Burnham-on-Crouch.* DANNY NICHOLSON*

Chapman's Light, off Canvey Island.

Chapman Sands lighthouse as depicted in a twentieth-century tinted postcard. MIKE MILLICHAMP COLLLECTION

Rowing over Chapman Sands in choppy weather.

by James Walker.

Chapman Sands, the mudflats and shallows off Canvey Island, have been notorious for centuries. Some historians believe that the Romans, fearing that ships would be lost after becoming stuck in the treacherous mud, had a warning beacon close to The Point. In later centuries, only the church towers at Prittlewell and Leigh acted as navigational aids over this dangerous stretch of the estuary.

Walker's iron lighthouse superseded a lightship which had been moored there four years earlier.

It was named Chapman lighthouse. The origin of the name may have derived from a farm called Chapmannesland which existed at Leigh around 1385. A chapman was also a medieval travelling merchant, and it has also been conjectured that the sands were named after those who sailed over them in search of their fortune.

The lightship had been brought there by Trinity House in response to representations made by a group of shipbuilders led by James Lamingask for a permanent navigational aid on the edge of the sands and to guard the deepwater channel in the middle of the river.

Chapman lighthouse with its hexagonal body stood 74ft high and was also painted red. It stood 800yards off the shoreline at Chapman Head at Sea Reach between Hole Haven and Canvey Point and was designed to lead ships clear of a danger called the Scar.

The lantern was fixed 50ft above the mean sea level and could be seen for 11 miles.

A clockwork device rotated the light which showed a white beam and a red flash every ten seconds or so. The red light was shown eastwards over the River Middle sand, and a white light in the safe channel. The light was shone white towards the west.

The lighthouse had a fog bell which sounded three strokes every 15 seconds.

The living accommodation was similar to that at Maplin Sands. A rowing boat suspended from the lighthouse provided transport to and from the shore when necessary.

The first light was shone in August 1851. Three keepers were employed: two on duty and one on shore. A steamer from the Trinity House depot at Blackwall arrived once a month to relieve the staff. Each man served two months on the lighthouse, with one month in three on shore.

The lighthouse is mentioned at the beginning of Joseph Conrad's 1899 novel *Heart of Darkness* as follows: "The sun set; the dusk fell on the stream, and lights began to appear along the shore. The Chapman lighthouse, a three-legged thing erect on a mud-flat, shone strongly. Lights of ships moved in the fairway – a great stir of lights going up and going down. And farther west on the upper reaches the place of the monstrous town was still marked ominously on the sky, a brooding gloom in sunshine, a lurid glare under the stars."

When Canvey Island took off as a seaside resort for Londoners, pleasure boats ran trips around the lighthouse from a jetty at Shellbeach. The captain would often hand a daily paper to the lighthouse keeper as his boat passed by.

During both world wars the lighthouse became a marshalling point for ships assembling in convoys. They would await the tide bringing armed escorts to accompany them to destinations overseas near and far.

One day in 1944, residents were startled to wake up and look out of their windows to see the waters almost black with hundreds of ships of all sizes, right across the estuary. They had no idea why. Soon afterwards, D-Day began on June 4.

Hitler responded with the V1 rockets, one of which fell near the lighthouse one evening. It sank into the welcoming mud and did no damage.

A much-loved landmark to mariners coming home, as for them it marked the end of the sea and the beginning of the river into London, its condition deteriorated to the point where it was switched off.

For many years, members of the Island Yacht Club sailed out on Christmas Day to bring hampers to the keepers.

In 1951, to mark the centenary of the lighthouse, the yacht club and Canvey Canoe Club presented a plaque to the Master of Trinity House.

However, the centenary celebrations were short lived. Because of the shifting mud and sand and corrosion of the metal piles, the lighthouse was found to be in danger of collapse.

A short farewell ceremony was held before the lighthouse was demolished in 1957 to be replaced by a bell buoy.

The General Steam Navigation Company's paddle steamer Crested Eagle *passes Chapman Sands lighthouse. This popular Thames vessel was taken over by the Admiralty during World War Two to be used as a minesweeper and was attacked by the Luftwaffe while assisting in the evacuation of the British Army from Dunkirk on 29 May. Carrying about 600 troops, she was set ablaze and run ashore, with over half of those on board being killed.* MIKE MILLICHAMP COLLLECTION

CHAPTER THIRTY ONE
THE INNER THAMES ESTUARY

FOR CENTURIES, the Thames estuary has been one of the world's busiest shipping lanes. Today, despite the closure of many of the docks in the East End, the estuary is still the second biggest port in Britain in terms of tonnage.

In the heyday of shipping, around 500 vessels a day would sail upstream. Today little commercial traffic passes above the Thames Barrier, built to protect the capital from storm surges.

The majority of traffic is handled by Tilbury docks, roll-on/roll-off ferry terminals at Dagenham and Dartford, and oil tanker berths at Purfleet, Coryton and Canvey Island.

Needless to say, there is an extensive history of navigation lights on both sides of the estuary, as well as the lightships and buoys in the middle.

This chapter follows our journey around the coast, and proceeds upstream from the coast of south Essex into Greater London.

The lost lighthouse of Mucking Bight.
MIKE MILLICHAMP COLLECTION

In 1851, a lighthouse was erected at Mucking Bight, 33 miles downstream from London Bridge. Mucking Bight or Flats is the name of a massive mudbank extending from Shellhaven up to Coalhouse Fort.

The lighthouse was built on piles and linked to the shore by a long footbridge.

It was made higher in 1881, being extended to 70ft and painted bright red, the colour of most of the installations described in this chapter.

It was damaged in the horrendous floods of the night of 31 January 1953 which decimated much of the east coast and claimed the lives of 307 people in the counties covered by this volume. A barge collided with the lighthouse the following year, and it was decided to remove it and replace in with a buoy.

Lying 25 miles downstream from London Bridge, Tilbury Docks were built in 1866 and are the first of the Port of London to be reached by incoming vessels.

Tilburyness once had a lighthouse of its own, built by Trinity House in 1892 near Tilbury cargo jetty.

It comprised a cylindrical tower made of iron and stood 35ft high. It became redundant when a new entrance lock for Tilbury Docks was constructed in 1930 and was demolished the following year. A light beacon has since undertaken its duties.

Two miles further upstream is Broad Ness, where the river loops around Swanscombe Marshes in Kent.

A lighthouse was set up at this point in 1885, to guide ships into Northfleet Hope from St Clement's Reach.

The tower was replaced with a new 43ft tall one in 1975 and converted to electric power six years later. Its light can be seen for 12 miles.

The light tower at Broad Ness. DAVID ANSTISS*

The Stone Ness light tower to the east of the Queen Elizabeth Bridge carrying the M25 over the Thames. KEN BROWN

Purfleet A.D. 1830

Purfleet's lighthouse as depicted in 1830, standing on the edge of a chalk abyss. MIKE MILLICHAMP COLLECTION

Stone Ness lies 22 miles downstream from London Bridge and is marked by a square 38ft skeletal lighthouse, painted red with a white band beneath the lantern. It marks the tip of a sharp promontory in the Thames south of Dartford Bridge.

With a focal plane of 36ft, it emits a green flash every 2.5 seconds.

The future of both Broad Ness and Stone Ness lights is in doubt because of river erosion.

Purfleet, at the head of Longreach, was the site of an experimental lighthouse built by Trinity House in 1828 on Beacon Hill 150ft above sea level. It was built to try out new forms of lamps and reflectors, and was intended to be as close to the capital as possible.

Experiments were carried out in 1829 to compare seven Argand lamps with improved reflectors. Experts based there also examined whale oil, spermaceti and seal oil, the only lamp

The Tilburyness lighthouse as seen in a 1931 photograph. MIKE MILLICHAMP COLLECTION

fuel available at the time. In May 1833, experiments were carried out with naptha gas to see if it could be used as an illuminant, but Trinity House took the view that the dangers were greater than the benefits.

Beacon Hill was so named because a warning beacon was set on its summit centuries before. It became one of a chain of signal stations from London to Harwich, for communicating with naval vessels. The chain saw frequent use during the Napoleonic Wars.

The lighthouse was of a similar design to those at Winterton-on-Sea and Pakefield described in earlier chapters. It had a house attached to it.

It appears that it was used only infrequently.

In 1840, Professor Michael Faraday, the great British scientist, physicist, chemist and philosopher who discovered the magnetic field, undertook experiments to compare English and French reflectors at Beacon Hill, along with the fuel oils used in lighthouses in both countries. Faraday had been appointed as advisor to Trinity House some years before.

As lighting apparatus technology advanced, such comparative tests became increasingly less useful. The lighthouse was eventually abandoned by Trinity House, and it was left to decay. The site became an anti-aircraft battery during World War One, but by then only the stump of the tower was left.

The great chalk pits at Purfleet extended to the point where they swallowed up the outcrop on which the lighthouse had stood. The chalk hill is now no more.

Coldharbour's metal framework lighthouse. DIAMOND GEEZER*

The experimental lighthouse at Trinity Buoy Wharf. MARTIN PEARCE

Coldharbour Point marks Erith Sands, and lies 17 miles downstream from London Bridge. A frame tower lighthouse was set up in 1885 at this point. Standing 38ft high, its light can be seen for three miles. Nearby, a metal frame tower stood on the end of Wallace's jetty at Erith Sands from 1960 until 1990.

Finally, we reach London's only lighthouse of conventional brick tower appearance, at Trinity Buoy Wharf in Blackwall, where the River Lea spills out its contents into the Thames.

The maritime use of the site began in the early nineteenth century when Trinity House established a depot to relieve lightships in the Thames. When Trinity House took over responsibility for all private lighthouses in 1836, the Blackwall site was used for repairing navigational aid equipment.

As engineer in chief at Trinity House, James Douglass instigated the building of workshops at Orchard Place. When they began operating in 1869, they had all sorts of skilled tradesman at work, from blacksmiths to chain makers and electricians.

The workshops also had their own plant for making gas from oil, and a training school was established in 1913 for new recruits.